TOP 100 Coffee RECIPES

A Cookbook for Coffee Lovers

A World of Books that Fill a Need

Fell's Inc.

Frederick Fell Publishers, Inc
2131 Hollywood Blvd., Suite 305
Hollywood, Fl 33020
www.Fellpub.com
email: Fellpub@aol.com

Top 100 Coffee Recipes

A Cookbook for Coffee Lovers

MARY WARD

Frederick Fell Publishers, Inc
2131 Hollywood Blvd., Suite 305
Hollywood, Fl 33020

For information about special discounts for bulk purchases, please contact Frederick Fell Special Sales at business@fellpub.com.

Prop/food stylist: Mary Ward
Graphic Design: Elena Solis
Photographer: Barney Taxel
Introduction: Tomothy J. Castle

Manufactured in the United States of America

10 9 8 7 6 5 4 3 2 1

Library of Congress Cataloging-in-Publication Data
Ward, Mary, 1940-
Top 100 coffee recipes / by Mary Ward.
    p. cm.
Includes bibliographical references and index.
ISBN 978-0-88391-163-1 (paprback : alk. paper)
  1. Coffee brewing. 2. Cookery (Coffee) 3. Coffee. I. Title. II. Title:
Top one hundred coffee recipes.
TX817.C6W8723 2009
641.8'77--dc22
                          2009024101

ISBN 13: 978-0-88391-163-1

Dedication

This book is dedicated to all those wonderful people with whom I've shared a cup.

A big thanks to San Francisco Examiner Food Editor, Jim Woods, who suggested I write this book.

Without the help of Donna Jean Morris, Barney Taxel, Vicki Heil, Donald Lessne, Brian Feinblum, Ted Lingle, Mike Carouso, and Tim Castle, this book would never have happened.

—Mary Ward

Table of Contents

Gentleman's Coffee Snack

Coffee and a bagel ... sure to refresh, revitalize and rekindle.

PHOTO CREDITS

Enamel tin cup from The Wilderness Shop, Cleveland, Ohio; wire glasses courtesy of Barney Taxel's Prop Room; antique books courtesy of Mary Ward; blue ceramic and white plate from Pier 1 Imports; brass plate from Antiques in the Bank, Cleveland, Ohio; pipe courtesy of Tinder Box, Cleveland, Ohio.

RECIPE CREDITS

Mocha Mugs, page 64

Quick and Easy Herb Crusted Bagel: in a small skillet, saute 2 tablespoons butter with 1 tablespoon finely chopped onion and 1 tablespoon freshly chopped parsley. When onion has browned slightly, place whole bagel (fresh or day old) into the skillet. Coat all sides of bagel, sauteing until it is crusty. Repeat with any remaining bagels. Cool, slice, toast and serve with additional pat of butter.

Introduction

This book is a celebration of the flavor of coffee. It joyously explores hundreds of possibilities for hot and cold coffee drinks, simple and complex, sweet and sophisticated. The author's expertise in blending flavors and aromas into delicious combinations inspires confident experimentation by the reader as well.

as beverages go, coffee is pretty new stuff. Coffee, in the form we know it, has been drunk for only a little under six centuries. Tea, by contrast, goes back a few thousand years, and wine may well be close to five-thousand years old. Once discovered though, coffee spread quickly, and today it is just beginning to challenge tea as the most popular beverage in several far-cast nations.

It makes sense then that people are still exploring the taste of coffee and how it gets along with other flavors. There may be rules about which wine to drink with which food but, so far, there are no rules about what to do with coffee. In fact, the tradition of flavoring coffee, or sweetening it, or mixing it with other beverages goes back to the first time coffee was drunk in the Middle East and Europe.

To this day, throughout much of the Middle East, coffee is served flavored with cardamom. In Vienna, coffee's first stop in Europe, shopkeepers served complex coffee drinks which included steamed milk, whipped cream, cinnamon, vanilla, and chocolate.

Probably the one thing most responsible for coffee's popularity is its gregarious nature: its boisterous flavor and aroma. There aren't a lot of flavors that coffee doesn't get along with. The recipe for Icy Java Mint, for example, is a surprising combination and a delicious drink.

Today, in the United States, coffee is undergoing a renaissance; Americans are rediscovering what a really good cup of coffee is and learning the importance of freshly roasted quality beans and proper storage and brewing. So intense is this resurgence that it has been predicted that by 1994, over one-third of the dollars spent on coffee in the U.S. will be on specialty coffee bought in the whole bean form. Of these sales, it has been predicted that over half will be flavored coffees, such as almon and chocolate raspberry.

among coffee experts, there are purists who would argue that coffee should be drunk hot, black and unsweetened. Mary Ward, though, loves coffee too much to let it lead such a grim existence. Through her many years of experience in teaching consumers and retailers how to brew the best cup of coffee possible, she has learned that coffee can blend successfully with hundreds of flavors and surprising ingredients. A surprise to me was Cafe au Vin, a recipe which dares to blend a port wine with strong French Roast coffee. It reminded me that the original Arabic word for coffee was, in fact, the same word for wine: Qahwah. Cafe au Vin brings out the fruity complexity of the coffee, and the coffee adds a fullbodied yet silken texture to this amazing taste experience.

Mary Ward also understands that everyone is not a coffee connoisseur. Her style is down-to-earth, and she presents things in a clear, easy-to-read tone that belies her enthusiasm for the subject matter. So, while the recipes are new and even sometimes surprising, they are also easy-to-prepare, with readily obtainable ingredients.

Before getting into the recipes, however, Ms. Ward takes the reader through the basics of coffee. Her second chapter is indispensable to anyone who ever wondered what was wrong with their coffee or how they would make it taste better. Later on, she gives guidelines for creating blends in addition to sharing a few of her favorites. She even shows you how to roast your own coffee.

One feature completely unique to this coffee book is a nutritional analysis at the end of each recipe, which allows diet-conscious readers to choose drinks to suite their own particular regimen. Not only calories are counted, but carbohydrates, fat, percentage of calories from fat, cholesterol, sodium, potassium, caffeine, and calories from alcohol if alcohol is used.

Ms. Ward also points out that all of the ingredients listed above, one of the most suspect, caffeine, is in moderation, probably the least harmful.

This book can be an important first step for any reader who has yet to discover the pleasures of a truly extraordinary cup of coffee. It will show you how to enjoy coffee much more and how to share it with your friends and family in new and scrumptious ways. But even if you've been reading everything written on coffee, I guarantee you'll find at least a few surprises, and some enjoyable ones at that.

Timothy J. Castle
President, Castle & Company
Former President, Specialty Coffee
Association of America
Author: THE PERFECT CUP

Coffee Blends

Blending and grinding different varieties and roasts of coffee is a great idea. It is discussed in several sections of this book.

PHOTO CREDITS

Turn of the century coffee grinder from Antiques in the Bank; enamel coffee cup courtesy of Roberta Hardacre; cutting boards from Barney Taxel's Prop Room and Ed nano; burlap coffee bag courtesy of Mike Caruso of Bernardi's Coffee Roasting; coffee shovel from Barney Taxel's Prop Room.

RECIPE CREDITS

...AND THEN THERE WAS COFFEE

no wonder coffee is so important; it's the first thing you drink in the morning!

Coffee...America's breakfast beverage! And it's no wonder because coffee is not only a tasty refresher; it is also a safe but powerful stimulant. Yet, when you sip a cup of hot coffee, you're taking part in a tradition believed to be only a few centuries old: 1425 A.D.

Prior to this time, coffee cherries were eaten in various forms. A fermented drink, made from a sweetened tea of brewed leaves and fruit of the coffee tree, was popular as an intoxicant and stimulant. This was also drunk freshly brewed and unfermented.

as coffee houses became popular in Arabia in the mid-fifteenth century, the idea of these particular social gathering places moved into Europe. Viennese and Italian coffee houses were popular by the 16th century, and by the 17th century, coffee houses were being introduced into the new world, particularly into North America.

Coffee has since become America's favorite breakfast beverage, as Americans drink one-third of all coffee consumed. The peak years for coffee consumption were the early 1960s, when 75 percent of all adults drank at least one cup a day. Throughout the '70s and '80s, consumption leveled off, but we are now seeing growth in the area of gourmet coffees, specialty coffees, and decaffeinated coffees. Currently, 100 million people in the United States are coffee drinkers.

The taste of the '90s? Although Americans drink less coffee, they are drinking better coffee. The specialty and gourmet coffee industry is growing at the rate of 13 percent per year in this billion dollar industry. Specialty and gourmet coffees use the most select of coffee beans which have been grown in exotic parts of the world. They are roasted in small batches and sold through specialty and gourmet stores. Generally, specialty and gourmet coffees are 50 percent to 125 per cent more expensive than canned coffees and according to coffee aficionados, "worth every penny."

Good coffee starts with good coffee beans. Here's a brief description of the growth process:

16

FROM BUSH TO BEAN

The coffee tree looks a little like a camellia...with broad, dark, and shiny leaves. The leaves are camellia-shaped and two to five inches long, lining up in pairs on either side of the central stem. The jasmine-type flower is small, white, star shaped, and placed in clusters at the base of the leaves. The coffee tree or bush is generally planted from a seedling, which has been cultivated from selected coffee cherries. In three years, the pruned and tended coffee tree will start to produce coffee cherries on a yearly cycle. A mature coffee tree can produce up to a pound and a half of coffee per year, depending on soil, climate, and general weather conditions.

There are hundreds of varieties of coffee trees, but 92 percent of these belong to either the Arabica or Robusta categories. Arabica beans are the select bean, lower in caffeine, flatter on the side, and generally more dense. Robusta beans are generally used for supermarket coffee blends, for internal consumption in countries where they are grown, and for instant coffee.

Coffee trees love the warm soil and balmy rainfall of countries located between the Tropic of Cancer and the Tropic of Capricorn. There, in the high altitudes, coffee thrives. Variations in soil, sunlight, and altitude produce changes in the coffee beans. Generally, the finest coffees are grown above three thousand feet, in rich soils, with an abundance of sunlight, and with soft, gentle rainfall.

The best coffee cherries are harvested when they are at maximum ripeness. At this point, they have taken on the appearance of a cherry. However, some Arabica and all Robusta beans are picked indiscriminately. This results in lack of uniformity in coffee product-some beans are overripe, some are underripe, and some perfectly ripe. Almost all coffee cherries are handpicked with a proficient coffee picker able to pick ten to twenty bushels of coffee cherries per day.

Once picked, the coffee cherries go to a local processing mill. Here, a process called pulping takes place. During this process, the coffee seed is washed, squeezed from the cherry, and sorted into sizes. In order to develop flavor, parchment coffee (as it is now named) is fermented for up to thirty-six hours in a water tank.

This being a critical part of the production process, fermentation is carefully attended by the mill owner. After fermentation, parchment coffee is hulled into the more familiar-looking coffee beans. These "washed" coffee beans are then sun dried. Although a lengthy sun dry period is preferred, many processing mills will speed the drying process by removing up to 8 percent of the moisture in mechanical dryers. Coffee processed in this way emphasizes the brightness of coffee flavors. When green coffee is ready for the market, it contains 12 percent moisture.

In countries with little water and lots of sun, another type of processing takes place. Called natural process coffee, the coffee cherries are pulped then spread to dry in the sun. This process results in coffee with an earthier taste than the above method.

Once coffee has been processed and bagged, it is ready for distribution. Green coffee has a shelf life of only a few months. During this period, it constantly changes: maturing, mellowing, fading and staling depending on the time of year, the climate and the particular coffee.

a farmer sells coffee to an exporter, the exporter sells to an importer, and the importer sells to a roaster. Once coffee has been delivered to an importer and again after delivery to a roaster, the coffee is "cupped" (tasted). Three small samples of coffee are identically roasted and finely ground. Next, seven and one-half grams of each are placed into three, five and one-half ounce cups. Boiling water is added to the cup and the coffee allowed to steep for one minute. With the cuppers' nose just above the crust or surface of the coffee, the cups are stirred with a stainless steel soup spoon.

This is called "breaking the crust," and a "burst" of aroma is emitted. Then, each cup is carefully tested by the coffee dealer as a means of quality control through taste. In the trade, it is called "slurp and spit." This is quite an interesting sight to watch… and to listen to. Incidentally, this process was developed in San Francisco by Folger's during the early 1900s.

Coffee, therefore, develops its unique flavor from a combination of type coffee plant grown, altitude, soil, amount of sun, and the method and quality of processing and milling.

BREAKFAST COFFEE AND WAFFLES

Start the day with freshly brewed coffee and a delicious Belgian waffle.

PHOTO CREDITS

Fork, ceramic cup, saucer, and plate from Pier 1 Imports; napkin provided by Dillard's; ceramic surface from Barney Taxel's Prop Room.

RECIPE CREDITS

Spiced Viennese Coffee, page 87

Quick and Easy Fruit Topped Belgian Waffles: Preheat oven to 300 degrees F. Place 4 frozen Belgian waffles on a baking sheet and bake until hot and crispy, about 10 minutes. Meanwhile, place 1 cup fresh or frozen strawberries (or other berries) with ¼ cup sugar in a blender cup. Pulse several times until syrup is blended. Top waffles with fruit syrup.

SERVES: 4

THE ROASTING PROCESS

The traditional American roast is very light as this roast tends to emphasize acidity and fruitiness. In American roast the body is less developed. Dark roasted include French, Italian, and Espresso with darkness varying widely from coast to coast. Gourmet and specialty coffee shops will carry coffee by categories such as country of origin (e.g. Costa Rican, Hawaiian, Sumatran, Kenya), by darkness of roast (French Roast, Italian Roast, Light Roast), and by flavor (Amaretto, Irish Cream). Quality coffee shops take pride in their roasting.

The coffee roaster has the ultimate responsibility in producing great coffees for the customer. Coffee is placed in a coffee roasting drum and heated, while rotating, at over four hundred degrees. The master roaster will know exactly when the coffees have reached their peak flavors or their "roasting points." At this point, the coffee is quickly cooled and allowed to cure for two to three days before being sold.

many Americans are interested in the roasting and flavoring of coffee beans. Gourmet and specialty coffee shops often carry green (or unroasted) coffees and recommend using a hot-air corn popper to roast coffee. If you roast coffee in this way, don't forget to cure it for two or three days before grinding and brewing. (I have included a recipe for oven-roasted coffee, see page 98).

flavored coffees are roasted, then sprayed with artificial agents to give them different flavors. Currently, flavored coffees are almost 50 percent of specialty whole bean sales. These coffees, often Colombian in origin, are easy to make and several are listed on page 94 of this book.

a coffee roaster may be a large operation which roasts several thousand pounds a day, or it may be a specialty roaster who roasts only a few pounds a day. Because roasting is an art, master roasters oversee the process with care.

SELECTION

at the gourmet coffee shop or in many markets, you will see coffee labelled one of two ways:

1) BY THE COUNTRY OF GROWTH. (Sometimes part of the name will indicate the area in which the coffee is grown, such as "Costa Rica Tarrazu." Other times, the name might indicate where on the mountain range the coffee was grown, such as "Guatemalan Antigua" or "sumatra Lintong.")

2) BY THE DARKNESS OF ROAST. (Italian and French refer to the darker roasts. Other names, such as city roast or European roast vary greatly from one region in the U.S. to another.)

Coffee is grown in Central and South America, India, Africa, Hawaii, Indonesia, New Guinea, the Caribbean, and in Arab countries.

CHART 1

BRAZILIAN:
medium-bodied, moderately acidic, pleasant earthiness
COLOMBIAN:
full-bodied, richly flavored, slightly winey
COSTA RICAN TARRAZU:
aromatic, heavy-bodied, hearty
ETHIOPIAN HARRAR:
unusual, very aromatic, winey, wild grown
GUATEMALAN ANTIGUA:
highly acidic, spicy, smokey flavor, very aromatic
INDIAN MYSORE:
aromatic, light-bodied, slightly acidic, mellow, scarce
JAMAICA BLUE MOUNTAIN:
aromatic, light body, mellow, mildly winey, very scarce
JAVA:
full-bodied, rich, acidic, slightly smokey, spicy
KENYA AA:
full-bodied, dry, winey aftertaste, acidic
KONA:
medium-bodied, mildly winey, sweet, aromatic, nutty
aftertaste
MEXICAN:
aromatic, mild-bodied, mildly acidic
SUMATRAN:
dry and heavy-bodied, low acidity, mellow, rich
TANZANIAN PEABERRY:
sharp, winey acidity, medium-bodied, rich
YEMEN MOCHA:
haunting chocolate aftertaste, winey acidity, sharp, grown
wild

Sources: Timothy J. Castle, Michael P. Caruso

CAFFEINE

Coffee contains up to 2 percent caffeine. An average cup of coffee contains approximately 160 milligrams of caffeine. Caffeine enlarges blood vessels, in effect, stimulating the cerebral cortex. After drinking two or more cups of coffee, one might feel a "speed-up" of the thought process, an increase in the association of ideas, a sense of euphoria, or an increased ability to learn and memorize numbers, concepts, and thought sequences.

Caffeine contributes to coffee's flavor. But, for some individuals, caffeine in coffee causes the "jitters." For this reason, we have included a chart (page 28) which notes the differences in caffeine levels. Most medical authorities find three hundred milligrams (mg) of caffeine to be a "safe" level. Note that just one cup of robusta coffee (the more inferior coffee) will provide that level of caffeine.

The quantity of caffeine in any given coffee will be reduced as that coffee is roasted to a darker version. A dark, waxy espresso, for example, will have less caffeine than a light Colombian.

CHART 2

how much caffeine is in a 6 ounce cup of coffee?

COFFEE VARIETY	MILLIGRAMS
Ethiopian Mocha	160 mg
Santos	160 mg
Minas	163 mg
Peruvian	170 mg
Mexican	170 mg
Costa Rican	170 mg
Kive Arabican	177 mg
Nicaraguan	180 mg
Cameroon	180 mg
Guatemalan	187 mg
Salvador	187 mg
Java Arabican	187 mg
Venezuelan	192 mg
Colombian	195 mg
Cuban	195 mg
India Malabar	195 mg
Haitian	201 mg
Robusta Congo	327 mg
Robusta Uganda	327 mg

Source: Kenneth Anderson

Leading health organizations have studied the effects of caffeine on health. Their findings indicate that caffeinated coffee, when consumed in moderation, does not pose a threat to health. However, if you have a history of heart arrhythmias, stomach ulcers, fibrocystic disease, or if you are pregnant, you should be especially cautious of the amount you drink or ... drink decaffeinated coffee.

DECAFFEINATED COFFEE

Until the mid-'90s, decaffeinated coffee was considered to be flavorless, bitter and a poor substitute for regular coffee. As the process of decaffeination has improved, so has its market share with nearly 30 percent of the specialty and gourmet coffees being decaffeinated.

When coffee is decaffeinated, the solvent used may be either water or a chemical. These methods differ slightly but the process is the same: the beans are first softened by steaming. As they swell to twice their size, they are placed in a chemical solvent bath for decaffeination. Successful decaffeination depends on removing as much caffeine as possible while, at the same time, removing as little flavor as possible. It has never been demonstrated, however, that any of the chemically processed coffees expose consumers to any health risks whatsoever.

In Swiss Water process decaffeination, hot water, not chemicals, dissolves caffeine while leaving in as much of the flavor of coffee as possible. The water is filtered through activated charcoal where caffeine is filtered out. More expensive than chemical removal of caffeine, this process is preferred by the many specialty coffee roasters.

In coffee taste tests, the average American may be able to detect a difference between Colombian Supremo, for example, and Guatemalan coffee. However, the same individuals often are hard-pressed to detect a difference between Colombian Supremo and Colombian Supremo DeCaf.

If you are concerned about your level of caffeine, you may want to try several other options: 50/50 blends; and Cafe au Lait, Cafe Latte , or Café con Leche. In these recipes, you'll have only one-half the caffeine of regular coffee. Also, evidence shows that your body will absorb only three hundred milligrams of caffeine at any given time. Additional caffeine will provide no additional stimulation. So...after those two morning cups of coffee (or whenever you've had three hundred milligrams of caffeine), try a decaf blend or one of the great hot coffee recipes in this book made with decaffeinated coffee.

WHAT'S BREWING?

In the remainder of this book, I'll present a complete description on brewing and serving a perfect cup of coffee. Then, we'll go on to more than one hundred recipes. They are well-tested and should inspire your imagination and spark your creativity.

as a coffee lover, I guarantee if you read this book, you'll start to brew a great cup of coffee. You'll impress your friends and business associates with delicious recipes from this book, and you'll find that you'll make Every Cup of Coffee Count.

"take time
to smell the
coffee."

Afternoon Sweet Snack with Coffee

Afternoon break: perfectly brewed French press coffee with Marzipan sweets.

PHOTO CREDITS

China pieces, Rosenthal, courtesy of Mary Ward. French press coffee maker from Bodun; hand crocheted pieces from Maruine Steinmetz's collection. Cutlery courtesy of Potter and Mellen, Cleveland, Ohio. Marzipan from Piccolo Mondo, Cleveland, Ohio.

RECIPE CREDITS

Café Au Lait, page 69

BREWING AND SERVING
THE PERFECT CUP OF COFFEE

For me, the perfect cup of coffee comes from seven scoops of fine grind, dark-roasted blend of Mexican and Costa Rican coffee per ten, five-ounce cups of cold water and brewed at two hundred degrees for eight minutes. Pour this hot brew into my favorite white, warmed ceramic coffee mug, add a little hot milk, and that's the perfect cup of coffee! When I brew this, my husband Joe has been known to comment, "The coffee tasted a little strong today." Joe likes a lightly roasted, 100 percent Colombian Coffee. Our daughter, Wendy, on the other hand, is a young wife, mother, and director of a day care center. She enjoys the economy of this week's whole bean specials. In other words, coffee taste and preference are personal: my favorite coffee may not be your favorite even if brewed perfectly. Economy and value play a big part in decisions about coffee brewing.

When I conduct coffee taste tests on television or in malls, I'll find celebrities as well as consumers preferring the taste of a familiar coffee over that of a more exotic one. Recently, at The Gallery Mall in Philadelphia, up to 50 percent of the consumers preferred the taste of the $3.29 a pound supermarket coffee over that of the $32 a pound, properly brewed Blue Mountain Jamaican Coffee.

If you follow all six of the following rules, you'll have the perfect cup every time you brew coffee. And, it will be a coffee to your liking. The perfect cup of coffee includes these elements:

1) CLEANLINESS: Daily and monthly routine to keep the equipment sparkling clean.

2) COFFEE: A coffee roasted (and possibly blended) to your taste.

3) TASTE OF THE WATER: Choose cold tap or bottled spring water.

4) THE EQUIPMENT: Consider the various types of coffee makers.

5) STORAGE OF THE HOT BREW: Pour brewed coffee into a thermos to keep it hot and fresh.

6) PRESENTATION / SERVING THE COFFEE: From disposable cups to elegant glassware.

CLEANLINESS

The perfect cup of coffee starts with equipment which is scrupulously clean. From coffee filter to carafe to interior pipes, each part of your coffee maker needs to be kept clean on a regular basis.

Before you fill your coffee maker with water, clean it well. (I use a solution of baking soda and water because soap leaves a film and an aftertaste.) A clean coffee maker will brew great coffee because it will not impart the flavors of yesterday's coffee. So whether using a drip coffee maker, a percolator, an open-pot system, or an exotic Cona vacuum system, first scrub all interior glass, stainless, or aluminum equipment with baking soda and water.

here's what I do: I keep a box of baking soda under my sink. In the morning, I simply wet a paper towel, scrub the interior of the carafe, then rinse it until the carafe shines. Once a week or so, I attack the exterior of the carafe with a stiff brush and the baking soda-water solution. This will clean out any residue of finely ground coffee from around the handle.

don't forget to clean out the coffee filter with a good baking soda-water scrub. The filter picks up residues and stains from the coffee. When you remove these stains with baking soda and water, you'll let the fresh coffee brew through. Rinse the filter well to remove any tiny grinds of coffee that may be lodged inside. This will enable it to work more efficiently and speed up the brewing process.

every thirty brewings (or once a month for most coffee maker owners), clean the interior of the coffee maker with a solution of one teaspoon white vinegar to a quart of water. You want to actually brew this mixture through the coffee maker. The vinegar will remove chemical deposits and buildup from the interior tubes of the coffee maker. This clean-up procedure will allow the water to pass through the coffee maker faster so that your equipment will work as efficiently as it did when it was new! Follow the vinegar rinse by brewing a cycle with clear, cold water.

In certain regions of the country, the chemical residues from water include iron, sulphur, lime, and other minerals. In those areas, ask your hardware store for a coffee maker cleaner-solvent.

Coffee 'n Cake

Flavored coffee is the perfect accompaniment to these elegant petit fours.

PHOTO CREDITS

Lenox coffee set courtesy of Al's Pottery, Cleveland, Ohio; silver coffee service from International Silver; hand crocheted tablecloth by Maurine Steinmetz; iced petit fours from Piccolo Mondo, Cleveland, Ohio.

RECIPE CREDITS

Chocolate Mint Coffee, page 99

When your coffee maker is spotlessly clean inside and outside, you'll be well on the way to brewing that perfect cup of coffee.

THE COFFEE

My twenty-six-year-old son, Jonathan, takes the art of brewing and drinking coffee seriously. A financial consultant based in Chicago, Jon tells me that the criteria for judging good coffee is as follows: swish the hot coffee far back into your mouth…past the sweet and salty taste buds on the tip of your tongue to those finely tuned taste buds on the sides of your tongue. Now, swallow the coffee. Count to ten. If you can still savor the lively and bright flavor of the coffee you've consumed, you've had a memorable cup of coffee!

Selecting the right coffee bean for your palate is essential. A local gourmet shop I frequent has sixty-four different blends and roasts of coffee beans. That's a different coffee every morning for two months. But with that kind of selection, how do you start to choose the right one? In my coffee taste tests, I've found that most Americans are conditioned to drinking lightly roasted coffee. So, I'd recommend that you start off with the light city roast and work through the darker roasts and blends as you begin to savor the bright and heavier-bodied coffees.

To make sure the coffee is fresh, I'd recommend you buy it whole bean instead of ground. To tell whether it's been freshly roasted, look for a date on the package. Most packaged bean coffees are dated. Purchase the most recent roast, as bag bean coffees go stale quickly after roasting. Some of the new bag bean coffees, however, are vacuum packed and have a longer shelf life, but I still wouldn't purchase a bag of whole bean coffee if it looks as if the product turnover is low (if the bag is dusty, for example).

If you are buying your coffee from a bin in a gourmet store or supermarket, ask "When was this coffee roasted?" The sales person should be able to give you a roast date even if it was roasted off the premises. Insist on this information, or don't buy it. Also, look around and determine how the gourmet coffee looks. For example, is it uniform in color and size? Is it free from external matter such as stones and twigs? Also find out how the coffee is being stored. Is it in an airtight container to protect it from air and moisture?

as you proceed through your coffee drinking adventure, you may want to start ordering coffee from a specialty coffee company. These dependable companies are master roasters who send their coffees to you quickly after they are roasted so you know they are fresh. For a discussion on thirty-six different American roasters, I recommend you read The Perfect Cup by Timothy J. Castle (Addison Wesley, 1991).

another way to judge freshness of the roast is to ask for a "one bean sample" of the coffee. Now, bite the bean. If it has a crisp bite and a strong, mellow aftertaste, you'll know it is fresh. If it is rubbery and bitter, don't buy it! Or, you might want to purchase one-fourth pound of several coffees... a 100 percent Colombian, a Kenya AA, and a House Blend. Then, perform your own coffee taste test.

after you've made a selection the next step is the grind. If you do not have a grinder, you'll need to grind your coffee at the store. Before grinding, allow the grinder to run for ten or fifteen seconds to rid itself of residues from the last batch of coffee. Next, grind your coffee to the finest grind possible without its going through holes in your coffee filter (fine grind if you are using paper filter liners). Then get it right home and into a well-sealed, air-tight, clean glass container. Store in a cool, dark place or in the coldest part of the freezer. For freshest flavor, I recommend grinding no more than one week's coffee at a time.

You may want to invest in a coffee grinder. There are two popular kinds: the blade coffee grinder and the burr coffee grinder. The least expensive coffee grinders are the blade types. The blades rotate much like a food processor or a blender. They are sharp and will pulverize your coffee beans to a coarse, medium, or fine grind. With a little experience, you'll know exactly the grind for your coffee maker. The advantage of the blade grinder is that you can add almonds, cinnamon sticks, roasted figs, and other additives to your coffee beans for new and different flavors. The disadvantage is the blade grinder does not grind coffee to the same consistency. In the same batch, some coffee may be very finely ground while some may be more coarsely ground. Many coffee purists insist that the blade grinder beats the coffee too much and this results in off-tasting coffee.

The burr grinder sends the coffee beans through two rotating wheels or burrs. This grinds your coffee to an even grind. Although more expensive, the burr type of grinder will grind coffee evenly and at several different grind settings. Some burr grinders have as many as eight settings from coarse to XX fine grind or espresso grind. Also, the capacity of these grinders is greater than for the blade grinder: you grind up to one cup of coffee at a time. The disadvantage is that burr grinders are designed to grind coffees, and you cannot use them for grinding almonds, cinnamon sticks, roasted figs, and those other additives.

There is some feeling among coffee purists that grinding coffee electrically will add heat to the grind and, thus, destroy some delicate coffee flavors.

So, many people still like to grind their coffee in an antique or other hand coffee grinder…or in a Turkish grinder. Although time consuming, coffee ground by hand is delicious!

In vacuum-canned coffees, the coffee is first ground, then packed in a can or bag. All air is removed. So, after grinding, the vacuum packing should prevent further deterioration of the ground coffee. However, vacuum-packed coffees often start with the more inferior blends that contain a high percentage of robusta beans. Whole bean gourmet coffees, on the other hand, are generally the higher quality arabica bean. In addition, because you are purchasing the coffee already ground, you'll have no way to ascertain the quality and uniformity of the coffee beans before grinding. In some vacuum-packed , ground coffees, the beans are burned, and malformed. Some even contain foreign objects such as sticks and twigs. All of these result in off-tasting coffees. When you purchase whole beans, you see what you are getting.

Still, having said all that, in my coffee taste tests, I oftentimes use a vacuum-packed ground coffee. Sometimes it is the least expensive coffee on the grocer's shelf. Time after time, up to 50 percent of the consumers will prefer the taste of the vacuum-packed coffees. Since coffee selection is a matter of personal taste, if you enjoy vacuum-packed coffees and appreciate supermarket savings, purchase it that way. Just remember, after opening, seal the can well and store it in a cool, dry place or in the freezer and brew it right for the finest flavor.

THE WATER

Okay. You've cleaned that coffee maker and purchased a really delightful coffee. What next? Well, since coffee is a blend of a little ground coffee and a lot of water, do you like the taste of your tap water? If you have off-tasting tap water, then you will have off-tasting coffee. You can remedy this by purchasing bottled spring water that is lively and oxygenated, ideally from a local spring. If you purchase bottled water, be sure NOT to purchase distilled water. It has no oxygen. Bottled spring water, on the other hand, will have bubbles rising to the surface, and this water will retain its oxygen even through refrigeration. One caution: distilled water comes in jugs similar to spring water jugs.

my five-year-old granddaughter, Melanie, was playing in the warm water at the kitchen sink the other day. She took a drink of the warm water and said, "Yuck." This was a reminder to me that cold water flavor is better than warm water flavor. Cold water has more oxygen in it and with that a more lively taste. So, if you like the taste of your tap water, let it run for a minute or two until it is as cold as it will get. Your coffee will have a better flavor. Also, the thermostat on most electric coffee makers is regulated to handle cold water, and the mechanics of the coffee maker work perfectly when the water is cold.

Should you store your water in the refrigerator? I don't recommend storing tap water in the refrigerator. The reason is that when water is stored, you'll see little bubbles escaping to the top of the container. These bubbles are oxygen. Again, for maximum oxygen, just let your tap water run for a minute, then measure cold water into your brewing system.

now, let's say you've cleaned up the old coffee maker, you've purchased some great ground coffee, and you have brewed that coffee with cold, fresh water. Your coffee is still mediocre ... what's the problem?

THE EQUIPMENT

Possibly, that old electric equipment is not heating the water hot enough. Perhaps, the thermostat is not working properly. Maybe it's just worn out!

DRIP COFFEE MAKERS

at present, many Americans who drink coffee brew it in a drip coffee maker. In a drip coffee maker, ground coffee is placed in the upper filter and hot water is poured over it. The brewed coffee trickles through the filter and into the lower compartment or carafe. The electric drip coffee maker will heat the water, brew the coffee, then cut back the temperature for storage. The proper brew temperature for coffee is right around two hundred degrees. At two hundred degrees, the right coffee flavors are extracted. A temperature lower than 180 or 190 degrees, results in a "muddy" taste to the coffee, and the temperatures higher than two hundred degrees result in a bitter flavor to the coffee.

If you use an electric drip coffee maker, you can measure the temperature of the brewing water. Here's how: take a clean oven thermometer and immerse it into your coffee carafe. When the coffee is brewed into the carafe, make sure the stream of water pours over the oven thermometer. After six to seven minutes, the coffee temperature will be at its peak, so look at the thermometer. You'll have a fairly accurate reading of the heat of your brew water.

If you use an inexpensive, non-electric glass drip coffee maker, water temperature is very important. Make sure the water poured over those grounds is just below boiling.

as important as the temperature of the coffee is the amount of time the hot water will be in contact with the coffee grounds. Many electric coffee makers, both drip and percolator, are known to take twelve to fifteen or even twenty minutes to brew coffee. By coffee purists standards, that's just too long for the water to be in contact with the coffee grounds. Coffee should be in contact with the very hot water for no longer than eight to ten minutes. After that, bitter flavors develop.

much has been written about the coffee makers with cone filter. In this type filter, hot water sprays over the grounds and is forced through one or more openings at the bottom of the cone…sort of a gravity pull system. Therefore, the grounds are penetrated more evenly by the hot water than a filter with a flat bottom. Most drip coffee filters utilize filter papers and require fine grind coffee. Although finely ground coffee offers better yield per pound of coffee, coffee purists would argue that paper filters absorb some of coffees' rich flavor. One of my coffee makers has a fine mesh filter, and though the clean-up is more difficult, this filter does make very good coffee.

Incidentally, if you are looking for the origin of a particular coffee maker, just check the product packaging. It will say, in large print, where the product was manufactured. It will also tell whether the product was approved by Underwriter's Laboratories (UL). UL specifies product guidelines for coffee makers. These specifications include a burn-proof exterior as well as interior electrical specifications. Do not purchase a coffee maker that is not UL approved.

New models of the electric drip coffee makers include a variety of features. Some have conveniences such as a drip stop which allows you to pour a cup of coffee during a brew cycle. Most manufacturers feature a one or two cup coffee maker which brews one or two cups of coffee in under five minutes. Several manufacturers feature coffee makers that store the coffee in a thermos. When purchasing a coffee maker, the first question to your sales person should be, "Which of these coffee makers has the hottest brew cycle … up to two hundred degrees?" and "How long does it take to brew a pot of coffee?" Sales personnel have been trained with this information. Let them guide and explain convenience features.

If you are purchasing a new coffee maker, I'd strongly suggest that you check it for comfort. The scientific name for the engineering study of comfort is "ergonomics." Check out the ergonomics of the unit. You'll want to practice lifting the carafe to test the feel of the handle. Is it a sturdy carafe handle? Is the handle attached well to the appliance? Will it pour? Remember, in a year's time, a carafe may be lifted as many as 8 times a day or 56 times a week, or 2,912 times a year! You want to make sure that it is easy and comfortable to lift.

THE PERCOLATOR

Percolators, invented in 1829, bring to mind images of coffee perking over the campfire or on the electric range. Who can forget the classic Maxwell House Coffee commercial with the jingle…"good to the last drop."

To Perk or Not to Perk:
Is That the Question?

The author enjoys an occasional cup of perked coffee. And today's percolators are a vast improvement over older models. They perk the coffee at a hot temperature with a brew time as short as four minutes. Properly perked coffee has a robust, well-developed flavor which is preferred by many people.

PHOTO CREDITS

Six-cup percolator courtesy of Farberware; cut glass jelly jar and Fostoria, Early American, crystal from Mary Ward; breakfast tray from Tuesday Morning; cup and saucer is Ansley (English) c.1940.

RECIPE CREDIT

Chocolate Chip Loaf, page 176

prepared in the following way: spray 12 muffin tins with non-stick cooking spray. Prepare Chocolate Chip according to recipe directions. Divide among muffin tins. Bake in a 350 degree F oven for 18 minutes or until muffins are just cooked inside. Muffins shown here are not glazed.

In a drip coffee maker, hot water is sprayed over the grounds. A percolator utilizes a pressurized brewing environment which acts like a piston in constantly circulating the water.

In the preparation for perking top-of-the-stove coffee, the water is oftentimes boiled, burning the coffee and resulting in a bitter brew. The first electric percolators, in the 1930s , were not much of an improvement as the brew temperature was too hot or too cool and lasted much too long (as long as 20 minutes).

Today's electric percolators are a vast improvement over the outdated models, perking at a temperature of 193 degrees with a brew time as short as four minutes. Properly perked coffee has a robust, well-developed flavor which is preferred by many Americans. Other advantages: percolators do not require paper filters.

OPEN-POT-BREWING

If you like a coffee which is richer and heavier, a top-of-the-stove, open-pot coffee maker may be for you. In open-pot brewing, coffee grounds are steeped in a pot of hot water, strained and served.

One popular type of open-pot brewing is the French Press, or plunger pot. The system utilizes a pot which is a narrow glass cylinder. Coffee and near-boiling water are put into this cylinder. Then, a tight-fitting, meshed screen plunger is inserted. After the coffee has steeped for three minutes, the plunger is pushed through the coffee, clarifying it and forcing the grinds to the bottom. Coffee is served directly from the cylinder. Although expensive, the French Press makes a rich, heavy-bodied cup of coffee. The advantages are clear: it is portable and easy. Full-bodied coffee may be prepared table side.

There are many more kinds of coffee brewing systems available from the functional Neapolitan flip drip to elegant Cona vacuum systems to the table-side Italian servers. It's a good idea to shop at department stores, gourmet shops, specialty coffee stores as well as mass merchants to find the coffee system that's best for your lifestyle.

STORAGE OF COFFEE

So, you've brewed that perfect cup of coffee. It is hot, fresh tasting, and memorable. How can you preserve that delicious coffee flavor?

Coffee is very temperature sensitive. Once brewed, it starts to rapidly deteriorate. Most electric coffee makers hold coffee at 160 to 170 degrees. However, even at this temperature, coffee will start to taste noticeably bitter in twenty minutes. In an hour, the coffee is very bitter. What to do?

First, brew only what will be consumed in an hour. If that's half a pot, then brew half a pot. You may want to invest in a quality thermos or in a coffee making system that brews into a thermos. One caution in using the thermos: make sure the thermos is glass lined. Plastic or other composition material thermos will impart off flavors. And with a glass-lined thermos, you are able to thoroughly clean the thermos with a solution of baking soda and water.

The design of the thermos is also important. The tall, slender thermos is designed to hold and seal in the heat from coffee, keeping it hot and fresh tasting for six to eight hours. The "roly poly" thermos shape exposes more coffee surface to air; coffee will cool more quickly in such a thermos.

But let's say you have coffee in your glass carafe, it was brewed one hour ago, and you've turned off the heat. Should you reheat the coffee in the microwave? Again, that's a personal taste. Cooled, reheated coffee doesn't taste very good. However, it does have all the caffeine; and if you're after that quick bit of caffeine, reheated coffee will give you that. Because coffee brewing is important to me, I want to make "every cup of coffee count." Rather than reheat old coffee, I use a two-cup coffee maker...one cup in two minutes, forty seconds...faster than my microwave would heat a cup of water.

PRESENTATION / SERVING

have you ever been invited to have a cup of coffee, then given a cup that looks like it was used for 250 years because it was so stained and dirty? Do you like the taste of your coffee in Styrofoam or paper cups? How about the plastic cups for the top of the car dashboard? The serving and presentation of coffee is every bit as important as the other elements in brewing.

first, coffee cups must be very clean. The coffee purists will wash coffee cups by hand, scrubbing out the coffee ring with baking soda and water. Allow cups to drain to sparkling dry. If you serve guests from a ceramic or silver coffee set, make sure the interiors are scrubbed well with baking soda and water. I've found that the dishwasher doesn't always clean coffee stains from coffee cups. For that perfect cup of coffee, scrub the cups with baking soda and water and rinse thoroughly.

For people who add accoutrements to their coffee, the perfect creamer is warmed whole milk or half and half. If you use powdered creamer, you'll have off-tasting coffee. For sweetening, I'd suggest simple syrup: a boiled mixture of 50 percent sugar, 50 percent water. For those who want a more continental flavor, stir with a cinnamon stick.

If you must drink your coffee in Styrofoam cups, make sure you rinse them first with hot water to remove any particles that could cause off-tasting coffee. If you have a decision between waxed cardboard coffee cups or Styrofoam coffee cups, the Styrofoam will deliver more true coffee flavor. Oftentimes, the wax from the cardboard cup will melt into the coffee.

My favorite material for coffee cups is earthenware. Earthenware washes well and really holds the heat.

a good coffee cup should keep coffee hot for fifteen minutes. Glass, ceramic, and plastic coffee cups and mugs do not hold heat very long. Dainty china demitasse cups and delicate bone china tea cups make lovely receptacles for coffee, but the coffee will simply not stay hot very long.

If you are using glass or other delicate materials, one good idea is to heat the cup before you pour the coffee. Simply pour hot water in the cup and allow to stand for five minutes. This will help the glass or china cup to retain the heat of the hot coffee.

another elegant presentation is the wine or Irish whiskey glass. I like to use wide-lipped wine glasses for after dinner coffees. They are easy to drink from and make a nice presentation. If you plan to do this, pretest the wine glass to make sure it will handle the heat of the hot coffee.

When you are buying demitasse cups, coffee cups, coffee mugs, or delicate tea cups, it's a good idea to test them before purchase. Some of the most beautiful sets are nearly impossible to drink from and to handle. If you test them, you'll know which ones work.

So, serve yourselves and your guests perfectly brewed coffee from sparkling clean, hot coffee mugs and you'll serve the best coffee in the area. Guaranteed!

a few years ago, my reputation was on the line. I was going through the brew steps for WABC's Live! with Regis Philbin and Kathie Lee Gifford. We were having a coffee taste test: Mary's coffee vs. Sy's coffee. Now, Sy was the WABC propman, and I had tasted his coffee. It was a hot, heavy-bodied cup made in a large percolator-style coffee maker. I was using a European-styled coffee maker with A & P's One Hundred Percent Colombian Whole Bean Coffee (inexpensive at $3.98 per pound). Sy, incidentally, used Maxwell House Vacuum Coffee at $7.98 for a two-pound can. The coffee taste tester was a coffee lover from Queens. Her name was Barbara, and she looked like a real coffee drinker. I had brewed a perfect cup of coffee, so when Regis said, "Is the best coffee number one or number two?" I was only a bit apprehensive. Barbara selected number one, my coffee. Barbara felt Sy's coffee had a "burned" taste. Sy's coffee, incidentally, was brewed at six in the morning for this nine o'clock morning show. Mine was brewed at eight-thirty. All personal preferences aside, I won that taste test because my coffee was fresher.

THE BREW CYCLE

for the brew cycle, measure good-tasting, cold, fresh water into your scrupulously clean coffee maker. Consider how much coffee you plan to drink in the next hour. Now, measure one tablespoon (or less) freshly ground coffee per five ounce cup of water. Turn on the coffee maker. The coffee should take no longer than one minute per cup to brew...for an eight cup pot, that's eight minutes. When the coffee is finished brewing, store on heat for one hour or pour into a thermos. When serving, pour into clean, hot earthenware or ceramic mugs. Serve with half and half or whole milk and simple syrup.

as to the correct amount of coffee, manufacturers generally recommend one scoop (just under one tablespoon) per five or six ounce cup of water. For many Americans, that's just too strong. In coffee taste tests, I find that seven scoops for a ten-cup coffee maker, or eight scoops for a twelve-cup coffee maker suits nearly ever taste. Incidentally, for my own taste, I use one scoop per five ounce cup of water. If you are measuring the fresh beans into a grinder, use a rounded scoop to compensate for a settling out of the ground coffee.

Get brewing but remember, every time you brew coffee, you will be performing your own coffee taste test! Make every Cup of Coffee Count!

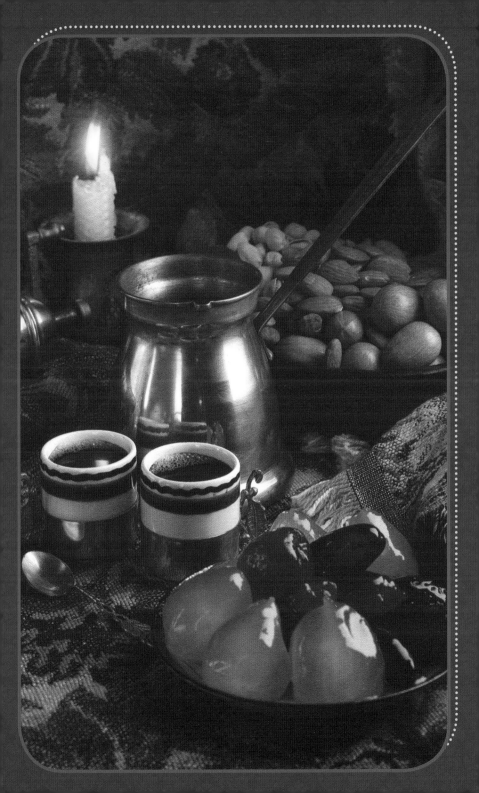

Turkish Coffee

This makes a fine, afternoon coffee.

PHOTO CREDITS

Ibrik courtesy of Barney Taxel's Prop Room; spiced fruits and nuts from Athen's Pastries and Imported Foods, Cleveland, Ohio; tapestry from Picadilly's in the Galleria, Cleveland, Ohio; candle from Wicks and Sticks, Cleveland, Ohio; candle holder, coffee cups, serving dishes from Antiques in the Bank, Cleveland, Ohio; brass coffee grinder from Arabica Coffee House, Cleveland, Ohio.

RECIPE CREDITS

Turkish Coffee, Page 77

HOT COFFEES

how many ways can you serve hot coffee? An infinite number, but here we have a collection of over forty-five favorite hot coffees. Any of these recipes may be made with your favorite ground coffees. Whether the coffee is decaffeinated, caffeinated, or flavored, all recipes will "work!"

from basic Scandinavian Egg Coffee and the rich tasting Mochas, to the aristocratic Italian favorites, you're going to find ways to brew hot coffees for your next Kaffee Klatch, for your next dinner party, and for those moments of relaxation with "a cup!"

as we start with this section, you will notice that almost all of the recipes contain a nutrient analysis. Many individuals today like to know nutrients in their foods so that they may tabulate their daily totals. The data for this nutrient analysis comes from NUTRITIONIST III, a software program from First Data Bank, San Bruno, California.

Recipes have been analyzed for amounts of calories, grams of carbohydrates, grams of protein, grams of fat, percentage of calories from fat, cholesterol, sodium, potassium, caffeine, and percentage of calories from alcohol (in recipes containing alcohol). Sources of information, along with NUTRITIONIST III, include the National Academy of Science's 1980 Recommended Daily Dietary Allowances (RDA), Bowles and Church's 14th Edition, United States Department of Agriculture's Bulletin #72, and individual manufacturer's data.

how to use this information? Always look at the number of calories…then the percentage of calories from fat. The USDA recommends a total diet containing no more than 30 percent calories from fat. In addition, you may want to count milligrams of cholesterol, sodium and potassium. Your doctor can give you his recommendations for your level of fats and cholesterol. RDA for sodium is 2200 mg and for potassium, 3750. The level of caffeine generally regarded as safe is 300 milligrams. Of course, decaffeinated coffee may be substituted for regular coffee in any recipe.

To reduce the calorie and fat levels in any recipe, reduce the amount of sugar and cream. Substitute skim milk for whole milk, and evaporated, skim milk may be substituted for cream. Frozen yogurt or ice milk may be substituted for ice cream in any recipe. In recipes containing alcohol, you will reduce calories and alcohol by heating the alcohol to a boiling point. After the alcohol has boiled away, the flavor remains with far fewer calories.

all recipes in this book have been triple tested, and are easy to read, and use. Also, almost all of the ingredients are readily available at your supermarket.

black forest**coffee**

- 8 ounces freshly brewed, French roast coffee (regular or decaffeinated)
- 4 tablespoons chocolate syrup
- 2 tablespoons maraschino cherry juice
- ¼ cup sweetened whipped cream
- 1 tablespoon shaved chocolate or chocolate chips
- 2 maraschino cherries

This is a coffee to serve instead of dessert. It is simple to prepare, and the ingredients make you think of Black Forest Cake! Use your finest china cups or Irish coffee glasses for an elegant presentation.

SERVES: 2

COMBINE coffee, chocolate syrup, and cherry juice. Divide into two warm china cups or Irish coffee glasses, six ounces each. Top with whipped cream, shaved chocolate, and a maraschino cherry.

Each serving: 233 calories; 18 gm carbohydrates; 2 gm protein; 19 gm fat (68% calories from fat); 33 mg cholesterol; 15 mg sodium; 109 mg potassium; 86 mg caffeine (made with regular coffee).

cafeau lait

- 2 cups hot French roast coffee (regular or decaffeinated)
- 2 cups hot milk, 2% milk fat

Our twenty-fifth wedding anniversary was spent in Chamonix, France, with our three college-aged children. In the morning, before skiing, we started the day with gulps of cafe au lait, croissant and baguettes. What a joy!

SERVES: 4

PLACE hot coffee in a hot coffee pot. In the second hot coffee pot, place the milk. Pour simultaneously from both pots into warm eight ounce cups.

Each serving: 38 calories; 4 gm carbohydrate; 2 gm protein; 1 gm fat (31% of calories from fat); 5 mg cholesterol; 39 mg sodium; 230 mg potassium; 139 mg caffeine (made with regular coffee).

69

café borgia

- **2 cups hot chocolate**
- **2 cups strong, hot Italian roast coffee (regular or decaffeinated)**
- **½ cup sweetened whipped cream**
- **grated orange peel for garnish**

here's an authentic Italian recipe. It uses the traditional, strong Italian Roast coffee and combines it with the sweetness of orange. Try this on a leisurely afternoon… perhaps before your next bocce game.

SERVES: 4

COMBINE hot chocolate with coffee. Pour into four, eight ounce, warm coffee mugs. Top with whipped cream and sprinkle with grated orange peel.

Each serving: 153 calories; 14 gm carbohydrates; 5 gm protein; 7 gm fat (51% calories from fat); 30 mg cholesterol; 88 mg sodium; 300 mg potassium; 72 mg caffeine (made with regular coffee).

café con leche

- 2 cups strong coffee (preferably Mexican)
- 2 cups hot milk, 2% milk fat
- 1 tablespoon granulated sugar
- 4 small sticks cinnamon

When Americans travel, they oftentimes find the coffee roast darker than they prefer. Adding hot milk will give this strong coffee a more familiar flavor. In all Spanish-speaking countries, and many other countries, by simply saying, "con leche," hot milk will be served. The Mexican version of Cafe Con Leche follows.

SERVES: 4

COMBINE coffee with hot milk and sugar. Divide evenly between four warm mugs. Place a cinnamon stick in each.

Each serving: 76 calories; 9 gm carbohydrate; 4 gm protein; 2 gm fat (24% calories from fat); 9 mg cholesterol; 65 mg sodium; 256 mg potassium; 70 mg caffeine (made with regular coffee).

café de olla

- 2 cups water
- ¼ cup Mexican coffee, coarsely ground
- 1 large stick cinnamon
- 1 tablespoon brown sugar

Mexican coffee, as in many Latin American countries, is boiled and strained through cloth or some other material. In Mexico, however, cinnamon and brown sugar are accepted additives. They add sweetness and spice. This richly flavored coffee is perfect for a mid-morning coffee break.

SERVES: 2

PLACE water, coffee, cinnamon, and brown sugar in a saucepan and bring to a boil. Reduce heat and simmer another three to five minutes. Strain through a fine strainer. Serve in large, warm, heavy mugs.

Each serving: 42 calories; 86 gm carbohydrate; 0 protein; 0 fat; 0 cholesterol; 18 mg sodium; 295 mg potassium; 278 mg caffeine (made with regular coffee).

caribbean**coffee**

- 1 medium coconut
- 2 cups milk, 2% milk fat
- 4 cups dark, rich coffee (Costa Rican, if possible)
- 1 tablespoon sugar

here's a rich, dark coffee blend with a tropical taste. This recipe was a hit at a recent Caribbean Cooking School I taught in South Florida. I like to serve it with fruit ice for a light dessert.

SERVES: 8

WITH hammer and nail, drive two holes into the coconut. Drain coconut liquid into saucepan. Bake whole coconut at 300° F. for thirty minutes to release coconut meat from hard shell. Grate fresh coconut (about one cup).

PLACE saucepan over low heat and combine grated coconut, coconut liquid, and milk. Heat until creamy. Strain, reserving both grated coconut and hot milk mixture. Toast grated coconut under broiler or in fry pan on top of range.

IN warmed mugs, blend hot coconut milk with equal amounts of hot coffee. Sweeten with sugar. Sprinkle with toasted coconut.

Each serving: 27 calories; 8 gm carbohydrate; 3 gm protein; 10 gm fat; 67% calories from fat); 5 mg cholesterol; 40 mg sodium; 255 mg potassium; 70 mg caffeine (made with regular coffee).

café mexicano

- 4 teaspoons chocolate syrup
- ½ cup whipping cream
- ¾ teaspoon cinnamon, divided into 2 parts
- ¼ teaspoon nutmeg
- 1 tablespoon sugar
- 1-1/2 cups hot, strong coffee (preferably Mexican)

here's my favorite Mocha. It's a spicy and rich mocha…a great pick-me-up for a cold, rainy afternoon.

SERVES: 4

PUT one teaspoon chocolate syrup into each of four, four ounce, warm cups. Combine whipping cream, one-fourth teaspoon cinnamon, nutmeg, and sugar. Whip into soft peaks. Stir remaining one-half teaspoon cinnamon into hot coffee. Pour coffee into cups. Stir to blend with syrup. Top with spiced whipped cream.

Each serving: 130 calories; 8 gm carbohydrates; 1 gm protein; 11 mg fat (74% calories from fat); 41 mg cholesterol; 17 mg sodium; 91 mg potassium; 53 mg caffeine (made with regular coffee).

costa rica**cafezinho**

- 2 cups cold water
- 8 tablespoons finely ground Costa Rican coffee
  (preferably from the Tarrazu region)
- 1 teaspoon sugar

Traditionally, the Costa Rican coffee processed for internal consumption may have up to 12 percent sugar roasted with the coffee beans. In the United States, Costa Rican coffee is roasted without the sweetener, and the flavor is delicate and bright. Incidentally, the coffee strainer, or Cafezinho, is sometimes referred to as the "sock." Serve Costa Rican coffee with light, crispy cookies as an afternoon snack!

SERVES: 4

MEASURE water into a saucepan and bring to a boil. Meanwhile, place the coffee into a strainer lined with several layers of cheesecloth or into a cafezinho bag. Pour the boiled water into a bag, holding over a receptable until all water has seeped through. Add sugar and serve in warm, four-ounce demitasse cups.

Each serving: 24 calories; 4 gm carbohydrates; 0 gm protein; 0 gm fat; 0 mg cholesterol; 16 mg sodium; 256 mg potassium; 278 mg caffeine (made with regular coffee).

caféeuropa

- 1 egg white
- ¼ teaspoon vanilla extract
- 1 cup strong, hot coffee (preferably dark roast)
- 2 tablespoons half and half

In this unique coffee, the egg white will float to the top of the cup with swirls of brown circulated through it.

SERVES: 2

BEAT egg white with vanilla until stiff. Divide between two, warmed coffee mugs. Top with coffee and half and half.

Each serving: 32calories; 1 gm carbohydrates; 2 gm protein; 2 gm fat (54% calories from fat); 6 mg cholesterol; 35 mg sodium; 106 mg potassium; 70 mg caffeine (made with regular coffee).

turkish**coffee**

- 1-1/2 cups cold water
- 4 teaspoons French or Italian roast coffee (regular or decaffeinated), ground to finest grind possible
- 4 teaspoons granulated sugar

If you don't have the traditional, long-handled Ibrik, use any saucepan. This makes a fine, afternoon coffee.

SERVES: 4

IN Ibrik or saucepan, heat water to lukewarm. Add coffee and sugar. Stir. Bring to a boil over medium heat. Pour off half of coffee into warm demitassee cups. Boil remaining coffee again. Remove from heat and spoon some of the creamy foam of coffee into each cup. Fill cups, but do not stir coffee once it has been poured. In Arabic, the foam is called "the face of the coffee"—and you lose face if you serve coffee without it!

Each serving: 23 calories; 5 gm carbohydrates; 0 gm protein; 0 gm fat; 0 mg cholesterol; 8 mg sodium; 136 mg potassium; 139 mg caffeine (made with regular coffee).

mediterranean**coffee**

- **8 cups freshly brewed, strong coffee (preferably Italian roast coffee)**
- **1/3 cup granulated sugar**
- **¼ cup chocolate syrup**
- **4 cinnamon sticks**
- **1-1/2 teaspoons whole cloves**
- **½ teaspoon aniseed, tied in a cheesecloth**
- **½ cup sweetened, whipped cream for garnish**
- **orange and lemon twists**

In this recipe, the spices enhance the deep flavor of the Italian Roast. This is a great coffee to serve after a light meal. Serve it HOT!

SERVES: 8

COMBINE first six ingredients in a saucepan. Bring to just under the boiling point over medium-high heat. Reduce heat and simmer until ready to serve. Strain into warmed coffee mugs and top with the whipped cream and orange and lemon twists.

Each serving: 109 calories; 12 mg carbohydrates; 1 protein; 7 gm fat (53% calories from fat); 17 mg cholesterol; 13 mg sodium; 160 mg potassium; 142 mg caffeine (made with regular coffee).

spicy austrian**coffee**

- 4 strips, 3 inch by ½ inch, orange peel
- 4 strips, 1 inch by ½ inch, lemon peel
- 20 whole cloves
- 4 tablespoons ground coffee, preferably (Sumatran)
- 1 quart cold water
- 2 teaspoons (or less) brown sugar

SERVES: 4

PLACE orange peel, lemon peel, and cloves into the bottom of a drip coffee carafe. Brew coffee as directed so that hot coffee drips onto spices. Divide between four, warmed mugs. Sweeten to taste.

Each serving: 22 calories; 4 gm carbohydrates; 0 gm protein; 0 gm fat; 0 mg cholesterol; 12 mg sodium; 181 mg potassium; 186 mg caffeine (made with regular coffee).

mocha mugs

- 1/3 cup unsweetened cocoa powder
- ½ cup sugar
- 2 cups hot, freshly brewed coffee (regular or decaffeinated)
- 2 cups milk, 2% milk fat
- ½ teaspoon pure vanilla extract
- ½ cup whipping cream, whipped
- ground cinnamon

ever get so cold you thought you'd never warm up? Well, here's an answer for heating up cold toes and noses. Make it up in advance and have it ready for apres ski...or after a cold, windy golf round!

SERVES: 4

STIR cocoa and sugar together in a saucepan. Stir in hot coffee and cold milk. Heat, stirring frequently, until it is simmering. Remove from heat and stir in vanilla.

LADLE chocolate mixture into four, eight-ounce mugs (or into a thirty-two ounce thermos). Top each serving with whipped cream, then ground cinnamon.

Each serving: 311 calories; 34 gm carbohydrate; 6 gm protein; 19 gm fat (52% calories from fat); 77 mg sodium; 367 mg potassium; 82 mg caffeine (made with regular coffee).

nutty**coffee**nog

- 1 tablespoon brown sugar
- 1 egg yolk
- ½ cup cream
- 1 cup freshly brewed, hot coffee (regular or decaffeinated)
- nutmeg

here's a very different kind of coffee…actually creamy and rich with just a hint of traditional nog flavor. It's a great recipe to serve with holiday brunch.

SERVES: 2

COMBINE sugar and egg yolk; beat well. In a small saucepan, heat cream. Slowly whisk in egg/sugar mixture and carefully heat to just below boiling. Remove from heat. Divide coffee among two warmed cups and top with cream/egg mixture. Sprinkle with nutmeg.

Each serving: 139 calories; 10 gm carbohydrate; 3 gm protein; 10 gm fat (63% calories from fat); 158 mg cholesterol; 35 mg sodium; 177 mg potassium; 70 mg caffeine (made with regular coffee).

orange**coffee**

- 1 orange slice
- 4 ounces strong, hot coffee (regular or decaffeinated)
- 4 ounces hot chocolate
- ¼ cup sweetened whipped cream
- 1/8 teaspoon cinnamon

I once served this coffee to food editors. It was easy to take the ingredients with me to the newsroom…and the flavors were appreciated by all!

SERVES: 1

PLACE an orange slice into a warm, eight-ounce mug. Pour coffee and hot chocolate over it. Top with sweetened whipped cream and sprinkle with cinnamon.

Each serving: 100 calories; 14 gm carbohydrate; 3 gm protein; 4 gm fat (33% calories from fat); 13 mg cholesterol; 96 mg sodium; 233 mg potassium; 72 gm caffeine (made with regular coffee).

coffeegrog

GROG MIX:
- 2 tablespoons softened butter
- 1 cup brown sugar
- ¼ teaspoon ground cloves
- ¼ teaspoon freshly ground nutmeg
- ¼ teaspoon cinnamon

COFFEE GROG:
- 6 strips, 3 inch by ½ inch, orange peel
- 6 strips, 1 inch by ½ inch, lemon peel
- ½ cup heavy cream, warmed
- 3 cups hot coffee, preferably dark roast

a special treat for a cold winter's day…delightfully hot and sweet. Make the grog mix in advance; it will stay fresh for several weeks.

SERVES: 6

TO MAKE GROG MIX, cream all ingredients until well blended.

TO MAKE COFFEE GROG, divide grog mix between six, warm mugs. Divide remaining ingredients between mugs. Stir well.

Each serving: 233 calories; 36 gm carbohydrates; trace protein, 10 gm fat (38% calories from fat); 33 mg cholesterol; 61 mg sodium; 211 mg potassium; 70 mg caffeine (made with regular coffee).

south of the border
coffee cooler

- 2 cups hot chocolate
- 2 cups freshly brewed coffee (preferably Mexican)
- 1 tablespoon cinnamon
- ½ pint whipping cream
- ¼ teaspoon cinnamon
- ¼ teaspoon nutmeg
- 1 tablespoon sugar
- 1 tablespoon grated chocolate for garnish

although this is a hot beverage, the combination of spices is certain to cool you off on a hot day. I love to serve this with cinnamon toast.

SERVES: 4

COMBINE hot chocolate, coffee, and cinnamon in a coffee carafe over a warmer. Whip cream with cinnamon, nutmeg, and sugar. Divide coffee mixture into four mugs. Top with whipped cream and grated chocolate.

Each serving: 283 calories; 17 gm carbohydrate; 3 gm protein; 23 gm fat (72% calories from fat); 83 mg cholesterol; 100 mg sodium; 234 mg potassium; 73 mg caffeine (made with regular coffee).

scandinavian egg
coffee

- ■ 4-1/2 quarts water
- ■ 1-1/2 cups regular grind, Scandinavian or Danish
  blend coffee
- ■ 1 egg white
- ■ ½ cup cold water

Scandinavians take special pride in making coffee this old-fashioned way. It is also a very convenient idea for campers. The clarifying effect of the egg white helps the coffee to sparkle!

SERVES: 8

IN a large saucepan (or campfire coffee pot), bring the four and one-half quarts water to a boil. Combine coffee and egg white, reserving the shell. Stir the coffee-egg mixture and shell into a boiling water. Return to a boil. Remove from heat and allow to steep for two minutes. Slowly pour in cold water to help settle the grounds. Strain, and serve into large, warm mugs.

Each serving: 10 calories; 1 gm carbohydrates; trace protein; 0 fat;0mg cholesterol; 14 mg sodium; 134 mg potassium; 139 mg caffeine (made with regular coffee).

spiced **mocha** mugs

- 4 cups cold water
- 2 sticks cinnamon, 1 inch each
- 12 whole cloves
- 8 allspice berries
- 4 ounces ground coffee (regular or decaffeinated)
- 1 cup whipping cream
- ¼ cup unsweetened cocoa
- ¼ cup granulated sugar
- 1 teaspoon pure vanilla extract

mocha is a popular beverage apres ski…as well as on the slopes. In fact, slope-side restaurants in elegant ski resorts such as Sun Valley, Idaho, feature mocha as a hot beverage. Here's a 1990's version of this old favorite!

SERVES: 4

POUR water into a saucepan. Add cinnamon, cloves, and allspice and bring to a boil. Simmer for ten minutes. Cool, then strain. Place water into coffee maker with ground coffee and brew according to manufacturers instructions. Whip cold whipping cream with cocoa, sugar, and vanilla. Pour hot coffee into large, warm coffee mugs, and top with generous dollops of chocolate whipped cream.

Each serving: 309 calories; 19 gm carbohydrate; 3 gm protein; 26 gm fat (73% calories from fat); 66 mg cholesterol; 37 mg sodium; 433 mg potassium; 292 mg caffeine (made with regular coffee).

spiced viennese **coffee**

- 4 cinnamon sticks
- 8 cloves
- 8 allspice berries
- 5 cups cold water
- 8 tablespoons finely ground gourmet coffee (regular or decaffeinated)
- ½ cup sweetened whipped cream
- cinnamon

dan Cox, owner of Green Mountain Coffee Roasters in Waterbury, Vermont, says this is a favorite way to keep warm through the cold, Vermont winters.

SERVES: 8

PLACE cinnamon sticks, cloves, and allspice berries into an eight or ten cup coffee carafe. Measure cold water into the coffee maker. Using ground coffee, brew according to manufacturer's instructions. Allow the coffee to steep for fifteen minutes after brewing. Strain into eight, eight ounce, warmed coffee mugs (or into a thermos). Garnish with whipped cream and a sprinkle of ground cinnamon.

Each serving: 17 calories; 1 gm carbohydrate; 0 protein; 1 gm fat (59% calories from fat); 3 mg cholesterol; 12 mg sodium; 124 mg potassium; 121 mg caffeine (made with regular coffee).

toffeecoffee

- ■ ¼ cup granulated sugar
- ■ ¾ cup hot water
- ■ 1-1/2 cups hot chocolate
- ■ 2 cups freshly brewed, strong coffee (regular or decaffeinated)

I recently took this beverage with me in a thermos for a spot on WIBC Radio in Indianapolis. Jeff Pidgeon, the morning disc jockey, appreciated the rich blending of flavors.

SERVES: 4

SIFT sugar into a medium-sized, moderately hot, heavy skillet, stirring constantly until all the sugar is melted and is a rich caramel color. Remove from heat and carefully add hot water, stirring until all caramel is dissolved and is maple-syrup consistency. Add hot chocolate and coffee and simmer to blend. Serve in heavy coffee mugs.

Each serving: 87 calories; 20 gm carbohydrate; 2 gm protein; trace fat (4% calories from fat); 1 mg cholesterol; 59 mg sodium; 153 mg potassium; 71 mg caffeine (made with regular coffee).

Truffles 'n Strawberries

Sweet tooth? Any mellow coffee will enhance the sweetness of the truffles and strawberries.

PHOTO CREDITS

Gorham mirror table runner from Tuesday Morning; silver bowl from International Silver with Delta Delta Delta motif; napkin from Pier 1 Imports; cups and saucer are Arcoroc (French); spoon is Farberware Stainless; truffles from Harrods (Knightsbridge), London.

RECIPE CREDITS

Italian Coffee III, page 165

White Chocolate Covered Strawberries: melt 1 cup white chocolate pellets in the top of a double boiler. Select 10 to 12 large, beautiful strawberries. Wash, dry and stem. Coat stem end of berries with white chocolate. Refrigerate until serving.

favorite**coffee**blends

many specialty and gourmet shops have their own "house" blends. In fact, most of the large roasters make up a house blend. The Coffee Company in Dallas, Texas, was willing to share three of their favorite blends with me.

for all three, mix and blend the beans before grinding. Then, follow any special instructions listed.

JOE'S SAILOR'S BLEND

This is a deep, rich blend with a mellow taste and sharp aftertaste. It makes a great breakfast coffee.

- ¼ pound Colombian Supremo (regular or decaffeinated)
- ¼ pound Brazilian Santos
- 2 ounces Viennese Roast
- 2 ounces French Roast
- ¼ pound Celebes Kalossi

JOE'S SPECIAL DESSERT BLEND

This blend may be served topped with whipped cream and a cinnamon stick to stir.

- 8 ounces Chocolate Almond Coffee
- 4 ounces Colombian Supremo (regular or decaffeinated)
- 4 ounces Viennese Cinnamon Coffee

JOE'S TURKISH BLEND

Pulverize (or grind to espresso grind) before brewing in an Ibrik (see recipe on page 61). Or grind to fine grind for use in automatic coffee maker with paper filter.

- 7-1/2 ounces Ethiopian Mocha Harrar Coffee
- 8 ounces French Roast Coffee
- ½ ounce ground cardamom

specialty**blends**

If your coffee seems to be a little lacking in flavor, try this: add 1/3 part of any of the following coffees.

To add brightness:	Costa Rica Coffee
	Colombian
	Guatemalan
To add body, richness, flavor:	Java
	Sumatran
	Celebes Sulaueise
To add sweetness:	Haitian
	Indian Mysore
For flavor and aroma:	Kona
	Jamaican
	Mocha
For a winey flavor:	Ethiopian
	Kenya

Blend with your coffee; grind and brew as for regular coffee.

low acid**blends**

Good coffee flavor is often accompanied by the acid from certain agents in the coffee. If coffee's acid is troublesome to you, try one of these blends… low in acid, rich in flavor and aroma.

> **Blend #1:**
> - ½ pound Java coffee
> - ¼ pound Sumatran coffee
> - ¼ pound Brazilian Arabica coffee (expensive)
>
> **Blend #2:**
> - 1/3 pound Java coffee
> - 1/3 pound Costa Rican coffee
> - 1/3 pound Kenyan coffee
>
> **Blend #3:**
> - 1/3 pound Colombian coffee
> - 1/3 pound Mexican coffee
> - 1/3 pound Indian Mysore coffee (scarce)
>
> **Blend #4:**
> - ½ pound Colombian coffee
> - ¼ pound Tanzanian coffee
> - ¼ pound Kenya AA coffee

50/50

mike McMahon, a manufacturers' representative in New York City, loves coffee "but the caffeine doesn't love me," says Mike. He suggests using one of the following 50/50 blends.

IRISH CREAM:
50% Irish Cream Regular Coffee/50% Irish Cream Decaffeinated Coffee

AMERICAN BLEND:
50% Costa Rican Coffee/50% Colombia Supremo Decaffeinated Coffee

KING'S BLEND:
50% Kona Coffee/50% Colombian Supremo Decaffeinated Coffee

AFTER DINNER BLEND:
50% French Roast/50% Amaretto Decaffeinated Coffee

AROMATIC BLEND:
50% Kenya AA/ 50% Colombia Supremo Decaffeinated

CONTINENTAL BLEND:
50% Celebas or Tanzania/50% Colombia Supremo Decaffeinated Coffee

With each of these, mix beans (or have specialty coffee store mix beans), then grind to a fine grind. Brew as you would for regular coffee. The caffeine will be reduced by 50 percent to approximately seventy-five milligrams per cup.

english**breakfast**
blendcoffee

- 4 ounces fresh figs (4-6 figs)
- ½ pound whole bean Mysore or Kenya AA or Ethiopian
- ½ pound whole bean Colombian Coffee

This is the unusual breakfast coffee served in fine English hotels. The unique flavor comes from the combination of roasted figs…and the Mysore (Indian) coffee. Mysore coffee is scarce, and you may replace it with Kenya AA or Ethiopian coffee.

SERVES: 32

WASH figs and slice into one-fourth inch slices. Roast at 300° F. until completely dry and crackly. This will take one to two hours. Blend together coffee and figs. Grind and brew as for regular coffee. This blend may be stored in the freezer in a tightly sealed jar for up to two months.

Each serving: 8 calories; 1 gm carbohydrates; trace protein; trace fat; 0 mg cholesterol; 8 mg sodium; 128 mg potassium; 139 mg caffeine (made with regular coffee).

new orleans**blend**

- 3 tablespoons freshly ground coffee (preferably dark roast)
- 1 tablespoon ground chicory (available in specialty stores and in some supermarkets)
- 4, 8-ounce cups cold water
- ½ cup hot milk, 2% milk fat

Chicory is the bitter-tasting cousin of the dandelion. Added to dark roast coffee, it adds a peppery tang to this full-bodied coffee.

SERVES: 4

BLEND Coffee and chicory. Brew as for regular coffee. Serve in warm mugs with hot milk.

Each serving: 28 calories; 3 gm carbohydrates;2 gm protein; 1 gm fat (24% calories from fat); 23 mg cholesterol; 34 mg sodium; 246 mg potassium; 104 mg caffeine (made with regular coffee.)

roasting your own
coffee

For the ultimate in fresh coffee flavor, why not roast your own beans? It's easy, as the only equipment you'll need is an expandable steamer. It's important to keep an eye on your coffee as it is roasting, though. Overly roasted coffee beans are flammable.

Preheat oven to 425° F. Spread unroasted, green coffee* beans to a single thickness over an expandable, petal-style vegetable steamer. Carefully place into hot oven. Roast for about ten minutes or until you hear the beans crackling. Coffee is roasted when the beans reach a rich, deep brown. Check every minute or two and remove beans when they have achieved the right color. If any beans spill onto the surface of the oven, clean them up immediately as they are flammable.

Cool roasted beans thoroughly and place them into a jar with a tight fitting top. Store in a dark and dry area. Allow the coffee beans to cure for two or three days before grinding. Home-roasted coffee beans will retain their flavor for up to four weeks.

*Unroasted, green coffee beans are available at specialty coffee stores, in some supermarkets, and through coffee roasters.

flavored**coffees**

flavored coffees combine a whole bean coffee with a powdered or liquid flavoring agent and ground nuts. Each flavored coffee will be a little different…and you may want to try combinations of your own. Please note that the water will go through the grounds a little slower with these coffees.

chocolate mint**coffee**

- ½ pound whole bean coffee
- 2 tablespoons mint flavoring
- ½ cup unsweetened cocoa

This lightly flavored coffee is excellent as an after dinner coffee. It may also be used in other recipes such as Mocha Mugs (page 80) or South of the Border Coffee Cooler (page 84).

SERVES: 16

IN a small mixing bowl, blend coffee and mint. Place on a baking sheet and bake at 200° F. for one hour. Grind to specifications of coffee maker. Place ground coffee in a medium sized bowl and blend with cocoa powder. Store in a tightly sealed jar in the freezer.

TO BREW: use one scoop (one tablespoon) coffee for each five ounce cup of water used.

Each serving: 45 calories; 3 gm carbohydrates; 1 gm protein; 4 gm fat (70% calories from fat); 0 mg cholesterol; 8 mg sodium; 188 mg potassium; 147 mg caffeine (made with regular coffee).

café amaretto

- ¼ pound sliced almonds
- ½ pound 100% Colombian coffee (regular or decaffeinated)
- ¼ pound Italian Roast Coffee (regular or decaffeinated)
- almond extract

This is a rich, dark coffee with just a hint of almond.

SERVES: 32

PLACE almonds on a baking sheet and roast at 325° F. for 10 minutes or until they are lightly browned. Mix coffee beans and almonds well. When ready to brew, grind to specifications of coffee maker.

USING one tablespoon (or less) coffee for each five-ounce cup, place coffee in coffee filter. To brewing water, add one-half teaspoon almond extract (for eight to twelve cups of coffee). Brew according to manufacturer's directions.

Each serving: 17 calories; 1 gm carbohydrates; trace protein; 1 gm fat (61% calories from fat); 0 mg cholesterol; 6 mg sodium; 109 mg potassium; 104 mg caffeine (made with regular coffee).

orange pecan**coffee**

- ■ ¼ pound pecans
- ■ ½ pound 100% Colombian Coffee (regular or decaffeinated)
- ■ ¼ pound Costa Rica Coffee
- ■ orange extract

SERVES: 32

PLACE pecans on a baking sheet and roast at 325°F. for ten minutes or until they are lightly browned. Mix beans and nuts. When ready to brew, grind to specifications of coffee maker.

USING one tablespoon (or less) coffee for each five ounce cup, place coffee in coffee filter. To brewing water, add one-half teaspoon orange extract (for eight to twelve cups of coffee). Brew according to manufacturer's directions allowing for two to three minutes extra for the water to penetrate the pecan flavored grounds.

Each serving: 18 calories; 1 gm carbohydrates; trace protein; 1 gm fat (73% calories from fat); 0 mg cholesterol; 6 mg sodium; 102 mg potassium; 104 mg caffeine (made with regular coffee).

coffeeconcentrate

The ultimate in excellent convenience foods is coffee concentrate. In fact, this is the coffee of preference by farmers in Central America. It will hold its flavor for months if you store it in a tightly capped jug in the refrigerator. It makes an excellent cup of coffee, and is the preferred coffee for cooking. Here are two methods of making coffee concentrate.

hot water coffee concentrate

hot water coffee concentrate makes a stronger and more distinctive coffee.

SERVES: 28

- 4 cups cold water
- ½ pound finely ground coffee

Brew coffee according to manufacturer's directions. (If your filter won't hold the full half pound, then brew twice using two cups cold water and one-fourth pound of coffee each time). Cool. Store in a glass jug with a tight-fitting seal.

TO RECONSTITUTE COFFEE: pour one ounce of hot water coffee concentrate into a warm mug. Fill with boiling water.

cold water
concentrate

If you like a mild, low-acid coffee, this concentrate will work for you.

SERVES: 16

- **4 cups cold water**
- **½ pound finely ground coffee**

PLACE water into a two-quart bowl. Stir in coffee so all grounds have been saturated. Cover and place the bowl in a cool, dark corner for ten to twenty hours depending on the strength desired. Line a coffee filter with filter paper and place over a one quart jug with a tight-fitting seal. Pour coffee, a cup at a time, through the filter into the jar. Seal and store in the refrigerator.

TO RECONSTITUTE: pour one ounce cold concentrate into warm mug. Fill with boiling water.

" **With enough coffee, anything is possible** "

Iced Coffee Interlude

Iced coffee adds romance to any quiet interlude.

PHOTO CREDITS

Iced tea glass, Williams-Sonoma; plate from Pier 1 Imports; pen, sterling silver by Angela Cummings; note, courtesy of Donna Jean Morris.

RECIPE CREDITS

Spicy Iced Coffee, page 126

Quick and Easy Lattice Peach Pie: preheat oven to 400 degrees F. Line an 8-inch pie plate with pre-made pie crust. Fill with pre-made peach pie filling which has been blended with 2 or 3 peeled and sliced fresh peaches. Dot with several pats of butter. Cut second pre-made pie crust into ¾ inch strips. Place half the strips horizontally onto the pie ¾ inches apart. Weave remaining strips vertically through horizontal strips. Seal and flute edges. Bake for 35 minutes until lattice pie is nicely browned.

ICED COFFEES

What do you drink when you've had enough hot coffee for the day…when soft drinks seem flat, and when you want a refreshing pick-me-up? I'd suggest an iced coffee. Iced coffee has caffeine for a pick-up (or iced coffee may be prepared with decaffeinated coffee). In addition, these iced coffees have other wonderful ingredients…nutritious banana shakes, delicious coffee coolers with ice creams, and refreshing iced coffees with fruit mixtures.

during hot weather, iced coffee also provides a cooling morning breakfast drink. But, no matter what the weather, I'm sure you'll find that these iced coffee recipes will please coffee lovers. As a matter of fact, some of my non-coffee-drinking friends appreciate the flavors of these iced coffee recipes!

make sure you brew strong coffee for these recipes. Better still, use one-ounce Hot Coffee Concentrate (page 102) or Cold Coffee Concentrate (page 103) and seven ounces water for each cup of coffee required by these recipes.

amaretto iced**coffee**

- 1 cup freshly brewed, Amaretto coffee (regular or decaffeinated)
- 1 cup milk, 2% milk fat
- ½ teaspoon pure vanilla extract
- 1/3 teaspoon almond extract
- 1 tablespoon granulated sugar
- ice cubes
- pinch of ground cinnamon

This coffee has plenty of flavor…yet is light and very refreshing. What a perfect coffee for a hot afternoon!

SERVES: 2

COMBINE the coffee, milk, extracts, and sugar. Place cubes into two tall, twelve ounce glasses. Pour coffee mixture over ice. Sprinkle lightly with ground cinnamon.

Each serving: 72 calories; 8 gm carbohydrate; 4 gm protein; 2 gm fat (30% calories from fat); 9 mg cholesterol; 65 mg sodium; 256 mg potassium; 70 mg caffeine (made with regular coffee.

banana**frostie**

- 1 ripe banana
- 1-1/2 cups cold, strong coffee (regular or decaffeinated)
- 3 tablespoons granulated sugar
- 1 cup vanilla ice cream

Bananas and coffee…quite a combo. And when you add the ice cream, you'll have a real treat…a lunchtime favorite!

SERVES: 2

CUT banana into chunks and combine with coffee and sugar in a blender. Blend at high speed. When mixture is smooth, add ice cream and blend at medium speed until smooth. Pour into two, twelve-ounce glasses.

Each serving: 301 calories; 48 gm carbohydrates; 3 gm protein; 12 gm fat (35% calories from fat); 44 mg cholesterol; 61 mg sodium; 448 mg potassium; 122 mg caffeine (made with regular coffee.

cafechocomalt

- 1 cup cold, strong coffee (regular or decaffeinated)
- 1 cup milk, 2% milk fat
- 1 cup chocolate ice cream
- 2 tablespoons granulated sugar
- 3 tablespoons malted-milk powder

here's a great cooler…a coffee malted! Try this about ten-thirty on a hot, hot morning!

SERVES: 2

PLACE all ingredients into blender cup. Blend at high speed. Serve in tall, twelve-ounce glasses.

Each serving: 274 calories; 38 gm carbohydrate; 8 gm protein; 11 gm fat (34% calories from fat); 43 mg cholesterol; 155 mg sodium; 466 mg potassium; 70 mg caffeine (made with regular coffee).

coffeefloat

- 1 cup ice cream (vanilla, chocolate, or coffee)
- 2 tablespoons chocolate syrup
- 1 cup cold coffee (regular or decaffeinated)
- 2 tablespoons sweetened whipped cream
- 1 teaspoon rock candy or other candy sprinkles

Coffee has a way of blending with ice creams so that it adds a mellow richness. Here's a great beverage… even for those who aren't fond of coffee as a hot beverage.

SERVES: 2

DIVIDE the ice cream between two, wide-mouthed, ten-ounce glasses. Divide the chocolate syrup and cold coffee between the two glasses. Garnish with whipped cream and candies.

Each serving: 243 calories; 25 gm carbohydrate; 3 gm protein; 31 gm fat (56% calories from fat); 46 mg cholesterol; 67 mg sodium; 241 mg potassium; 76 mg caffeine (made with regular coffee).

coffeefrostie

- ½ cup instant nonfat dry milk
- ½ cup ice water
- ¼ cup granulated sugar
- ½ cup strong, cold coffee (regular or decaffeinated)
- 1 pint coffee ice cream, softened

here's a recipe that will go with breakfast, lunch or dinner. It's light, yet sweet and creamy. It's an especially nice way to use flavored coffees such as Irish Cream Coffee or Amaretto Flavored Coffee.

SERVES: 4

CHILL beater blades and small bowl of an electric mixer. Measure instant dry milk into chilled bowl. Add ice water; blend. Beat at high speed until soft peaks form (about five minutes). Combine sugar and cold coffee. Add slowly, continuing to beat. Turn to low speed. Add ice cream, about one-quarter of it at time, beating after each addition until blended. Pour into four, ten-ounce stemmed glasses. Serve with sipping straws.

Each serving: 251 calories; 33 gm carbohydrates; 5 gm protein; 12 gm fat (42% calories from fat); 46 mg cholesterol; 101 mg sodium; 272 mg potassium; 18 mg caffeine (made with regular coffee).

continental**coffee cooler**

- 1-1/2 cups freshly brewed, French roast coffee
- ½ teaspoon Agnostura bitters
- ½ teaspoon pure vanilla extract
- 1-1/2 tablespoons sugar
- 1 cup cold club soda
- 4 orange sections

When I first tried this recipe, I was thrilled at the way the flavors seemed to sparkle. This is elegant…and has only twenty-five calories per serving!

SERVES: 4

MIX together coffee, bitters, vanilla, and sugar. Pour into four, ten-ounce glasses. Add ice cubes to fill within two inches of the top. Top with club soda and orange sections.

Each serving: 25 calories; 6 gm carbohydrate; 0 protein; 0 fat; 0 cholesterol; 28 mg sodium; 73 mg potassium; 51 mg caffeine (made with regular coffee).

cool**coffee**tropicana

- 4 cups freshly brewed, French Roast Coffee
- 1 cup milk, 2% milk fat
- 1 teaspoon rum flavoring
- 1 tablespoon simple syrup *
- 3 cups cracked ice
- 1 cup cold sparkling water or club soda

This iced coffee is a summertime favorite at Green Mountain Coffee Roasters in Waterbury, Vermont. They sell lots of tall glasses of this cooling confection!

SERVES: 6

COMBINE coffee, milk, rum flavoring, and simple syrup. Chill. Place one-half cup cracked ice in each of six tall glasses. Pour in coffee mixture. Top with sparkling water.

*TO MAKE simple syrup: simmer one-half cup sugar with one-half cup water for five minutes, until all sugar is dissolved. Cool. Store in a covered jar in the refrigerator. Simple syrup will keep indefinitely. It is a great sweetener for coffee drinks.

Each serving: 36 calories; 5 gm carbohydrate; 2 gm protein; 1 gm fat (22% calories from fat); 3 mg cholesterol; 38 mg sodium; 165 mg potassium; 75 mg caffeine (made with regular coffee).

iced**cardamom**delight

- 1 teaspoon cardamom seeds
- 4 cups cold water
- 6 scoops (or 6 tablespoons) ground coffee
  (preferably Scandinavian or Danish blend)
- ½ cup fresh or canned pineapple chunks
- 18 maraschino cherries
- 6 wooden skewers, 4 inches long

One more super, low-calorie recipe (under thirty calories). The Scandinavian blend of coffee is wonderful in this recipe. Add pineapple and cherry skewers for a delightful presentation.

SERVES: 6

IN a saucepan, blend cardamom seeds and water. Bring to a boil and boil for five minutes. Cool water for one hour in refrigerator. Strain water into the water reservoir of coffee maker and brew ground coffee according to manufacturer's direction. Fill six tall, ten-ounce, heat-resistant glasses full of ice. Pour hot coffee over and garnish with pineapple chunks and maraschino cherries which have been skewered onto wooden skewers.

Each serving: 29 calories; 6 gm carbohydrate; 0 protein; .5 gm fat (3% calories from fat); 0 cholesterol; 8 mg sodium; 191 mg potassium; 136 mg caffeine (made with regular coffee).

iced**mocha**with mint

- **2 tablespoons chocolate syrup**
- **¾ cup freshly brewed coffee (regular or decaffeinated)**
- **¼ cup milk**
- **dash of mint extract**
- **1 scoop crushed ice**
- **mint leaf for garnish**

This recipe is a great pick-me-up for late afternoon. It was served to me several years ago, and I've loved it ever since. This is written for a single serving but can be expanded accordingly.

SERVES: 1

IN a blender, combine chocolate syrup, coffee, milk, mint, and crushed ice. Blend until frothy. Pour into a tall glass and garnish with a mint leaf and straw.

Each serving: 123 calories; 26 gm carbohydrate; 3 gm protein; 2 gm fat (11% calories from fat); 5 mg cholesterol; 62 mg sodium; 319 mg potassium; 102 mg caffeine (made with regular coffee).

iced**slenderella**

- Ice cubes
- 1-1/2 cups strong, cool coffee (regular or
  decaffeinated)
- 1 tablespoon granulated sugar

This is a basic iced coffee recipe. It is refreshing, low in calories, and extremely easy to prepare.

SERVES: 4

FILL blender cup half full of ice cubes. Add coffee and sugar. Blend until thick and foamy. Pour into four tall glasses.

Each serving: 29 calories; 7 gm carbohydrate; 0 protein; 0 gm fat; 0 cholesterol; 6 mg sodium; 102 mg potassium; 51 mg caffeine (made with regular coffee).

iced**toffee**

- 1 Heath Bar, 1-3/16 ounces
- 2 cups vanilla ice cream
- ½ cup cold, strong coffee (regular or decaffeinated)

here's a great recipe for anyone who loves toffee. This is the perfect dessert beverage.

SERVES: 2

BREAK Heath Bar into four pieces. Place in blender cup with softened ice cream and coffee. Blend on high until candy is blended smooth and the mixture is thick. Pour into two, twelve-ounce glasses. Serve with a spoon.

Each serving: 448 calories; 39 gm carbohydrate; 7 gm protein; 31 gm fat (60% calories from fat); 88 mg cholesterol; 119 mg sodium; 341 mg potassium; 34 mg caffeine (made with regular coffee).

icy**java**mint

- 4 cups cold coffee (regular or decaffeinated)
- ½ cup simple syrup (page 114)
- ½ cup half and half
- ½ teaspoon mint extract
- 2 cups crushed ice
- ½ cup sweetened whipped cream
- mint sprigs for garnish

This is a drink for mint lovers. It is cooling, refreshing… yet a very different kind of treat. Try this after a light, salad luncheon on a hot, hot day.

SERVES: 4

MIX together coffee, simple syrup, half and half, and mint extract. Divide into four, ten-ounce glasses which are partially filled with crushed ice. Top with whipped cream and a mint sprig.

Each serving: 111 calories; 15 gm carbohydrate; 1 gm protein; 5 gm fat (42% calories from fat); 17 mg cholesterol; 30 mg sodium; 186 mg potassium; 136 mg caffeine (made with regular coffee).

icy**jazzberry**java

- 1 package frozen raspberries (10 ounces)
- ½ cup granulated sugar
- ½ cup water
- 10 cups cold coffee (regular or decaffeinated)
- 1 pint half and half
- 1 cup sweetened whipped cream
- 10 mint sprigs
- 10 whole raspberries

Green Mountain Coffee Roasters in Waterbury, Vermont, like to create coffees with appeal to college students. When my son, Bob, was in college at The University of Vermont, this was practically his favorite beverage.

SERVES: 10

PUREE frozen raspberries, sugar, and water in a blender cup. Strain mixture into a large mixing bowl. Add coffee and half and half. Blend well. Ladle into ten, twelve-ounce glasses partially filled with cracked ice. Top with whipped cream, mint sprigs, and whole raspberries.

Each serving: 155 calories; 22 gm carbohydrate; 2 gm protein; 7 gm fat (40% calories from fat); 23 mg cholesterol; 36 mg sodium; 247 mg potassium; 136 mg caffeine (made with regular coffee).

midnight**sun**cooler

- 2 cups Scandinavian Blend (or Danish Blend) Coffee, brewed double strength
- 1 teaspoon pure Dutch cocoa
- 1 teaspoon vanilla extract
- 4 teaspoons sugar
- 4 ice cubes
- 1 cup vanilla ice cream
- 2 strawberries for garnish

during the first year's business at Village Roaster, in Lakewood, Colorado, Mary Ann and Gary Mencimer were looking for ways to stimulate coffee sales during the heat of the summer. This recipe was a hit!

SERVES: 2

CHILL freshly made coffee. Rapidly froth all ingredients (except strawberries) in blender. Serve in chilled Irish coffee glasses garnished with a strawberry on the rim of the glass.

Each serving: 190 calories; 26 gm carbohydrate; 3 gm protein; 8 gm fat (39% calories from fat); 30 mg cholesterol; 74 mg sodium; 400 mg potassium; 280 mg caffeine (made with regular coffee).

mochamist

- 2-1/2 cups strong, cold coffee (regular or decaffeinated)
- 5 tablespoons chocolate syrup
- 1 pint coffee ice cream

here's a frosty beverage which may just be better than a milk shake. It's rich and chocolatey.

SERVES: 4

PLACE all ingredients in blender and blend until smooth. Pour into four tall glasses.

Each serving: 231 calories; 31 gm carbohydrate; 3 gm protein; 12 gm fat (45% calories from fat); 44 mg cholesterol; 72 mg sodium; 261 mg potassium; 155 mg caffeine (made with regular coffee).

mocha**silk**soda

- 1 pint chocolate ice cream
- 1 pint vanilla ice cream
- 1 pint coffee ice cream
- 4 cups freshly brewed, hot coffee (regular or decaffeinated)
- ½ cup sweetened whipped cream

Is this a dessert…or an iced coffee? Either way, you'll spoon this satiny smooth cooler at the beginning, but you'll end up by sipping it through a straw! To reduce calories, Mocha Silk Soda may be made with frozen yogurt or ice milk.

SERVES: 4

LADLE one scoop (one-half cup) of each ice cream into four, large, heat-proof soda glasses. Pour one cup hot coffee over each glass. Top with whipped cream.

Each serving (made with ice cream): 550 calories; 50 gm carbohydrate; 6 gm protein; 37 gm fat (60% calories from fat); 137 mg cholesterol; 179 mg sodium; 478 mg potassium; 136 mg caffeine (made with regular coffee).

mock **de menthe**

- 1 cup cold, strong coffee (regular or decaffeinated)
- 1 cup vanilla ice cream
- 1 cup mint ice cream
- 1 teaspoon mint extract
- mint leaves for garnish

This tastes like a grasshopper…smooth, and mellow. Yet, this version has that secret ingredient, COFFEE!

SERVES: 4

PLACE coffee, ice creams, and mint extract into blender cup. Blend until smooth. Pour into four champagne or wine glasses. Top with mint leaves.

Each serving: 176 calories; 16 gm carbohydrate; 2 gm protein; 12 gm fat (59% calories from fat); 44 mg cholesterol; 56 mg sodium; 144 mg potassium; 35 mg caffeine (made with regular coffee).

peanut butter
jelly float

- 1 cup cold, strong coffee (regular or decaffeinated)
- 1 cup milk, 2% milk fat
- 1 heaping tablespoon smooth style peanut butter
- 4 tablespoons strawberry jelly

This drink has a smooth, delicious, nutty flavor with just a hint of sweetness for the kid inside us all.

SERVES: 2

PLACE all ingredients in a blender cup. Blend at high speed until foamy. Pour into two, eight-ounce glasses.

Each serving: 220 calories; 34 gm carbohydrates; 7 gm protein; 7 gm fat (26% carbohydrates from fat); 10 mg cholesterol; 120 mg sodium; 374 mg potassium; 70 mg caffeine (made with regular coffee).

spicy**iced**coffee

- 3 cups freshly brewed, Mexican coffee
- 2 cinnamon sticks
- 4 cloves
- 4 allspice berries
- lemon peel for garnish

Try using Mexican Grown Coffee for this iced treat. The flavors blend well…a real must for iced coffee lovers!

SERVES: 4

POUR coffee over cinnamon sticks, cloves, and allspice berries. Let stand for one hour. Pour mixture over ice which has been divided between four tall glasses. Garnish with lemon peel.

Each serving: 10 calories; trace gm carbohydrates; 0 gm protein; 0 gm fat; 0 mg cholesterol; 0 mg sodium; 0 mg potassium; 122 mg caffeine (made with regular coffee).

tropical**mocha**smoothie

- 1 ripe banana
- 1 cup milk, 2% milk fat
- 2 tablespoons chocolate syrup
- ½ cup cold coffee
- chocolate curls for garnish

here's a great way to have breakfast in a glass. It's creamy, flavorful, and only 166 calories per serving.

SERVES: 2

COMBINE first four ingredients into a blender cup. Blend until smooth and creamy. Pour over crushed ice into a tall cooler glass. Garnish with chocolate curls and serve with a straw.

Each serving: 166 calories; 32 mg carbohydrate; 6 gm protein; 3 gm fat (15% calories from fat); 10 mg cholesterol; 85 mg sodium; 546 mg potassium; 37 mg caffeine (made with regular coffee).

café mazagran

- 1 cup crushed ice
- ½ cup cool, strong brewed coffee, preferably Mexican or Costa Rican (regular or decaffeinated)
- 1 teaspoon simple syrup (page 114)
- ½ cup cold club soda

a very refreshing beverage, this is best made with a Latin American coffee such as Mexican or Costa Rican.

SERVES: 1

FILL a twelve-ounce glass with crushed ice. Add coffee and stir in syrup. Slowly pour in club soda.

Each serving: 12 calories; 2 gm carbohydrate; 0 gm protein; 0 gm fat; 0 mg cholesterol; 28 mg sodium; 64 mg potassium; 70 mg caffeine (made with regular coffee).

spiced citrus
iced coffee

- 1 strip, 2 by ½ inch, lemon peel
- 1 strip, 4 by ½ inch, orange peel
- 12 whole cloves
- 4 tablespoons light roast coffee such as Colombian (regular or decaffeinated)
- 4 cups water
- 4 teaspoons simple syrup (page 114)
- 4 tablespoons half and half

This full-flavored coffee will become even spicier as it cures in the refrigerator.

SERVES: 6

PLACE lemon strip, orange strip, and cloves into a coffee carafe. Brew coffee according to manufacturers' directions. Cool and store in a sealed jug in the refrigerator for twelve hours. To serve: add simple syrup, half and half and pour into six tall, twelve-ounce glasses.

Each serving: 24 calories; 2 gm carbohydrate; trace protein; 1 gm fat (50% calories from fat); 4 mg cholesterol; 9 mg sodium; 98 mg potassium; 93 mg caffeine (made with regular coffee).

smooth and creamy
iced cafe

- 1 cup strong, cold coffee (regular or decaffeinated)
- 4 teaspoons confectioners' sugar
- 1 cup half and half
- 3 cups crushed ice

Call this a creamy slush with a milk coffee flavor. Or, just call it delicious.

SERVES: 4

PLACE all ingredients into a blender cup. Blend until smooth. Pour into four, ten-ounce glasses.

Each serving: 89 calories, 5 gm carbohydrate, 2 gm protein; 7 gm fat (70% calories from fat); 22 mg cholesterol; 27 mg sodium; 111 mg potassium; 35 mg caffeine (made with regular coffee).

Espresso Express

For espresso, an electric or top-of-the-stove espresso maker is essential. This authentic, Italian espresso maker was purchased by my son, Bob, during his year-long study in Florence and Venice. On a daily basis his Italian family used an espresso maker just like this.

PHOTO CREDITS

Espresso maker, courtesy of Bob Ward; espresso cups are bone china courtesy of Al's Pottery, Cleveland, Ohio. Marble pieces are from Barney Taxel's Prop Room; teaspoon courtesy of Maurine Steinmetz.

RECIPE CREDIT

Authentic Espresso or Cappuccino,
page 135

ESPRESSO AND CAPPUCCINO

If flavored and specialty coffees were the beverages of the '80s, then espresso and cappuccino are truly the beverages of the '90s. The rich flavor of espresso and the smooth taste of cappuccino are perfect afternoon pick-ups.

Perhaps none of the coffee beverages are as misunderstood as the names of these beverages. It's really very simple. Espresso is finely ground, dark-roast coffee which has been made under pressure and steam. Cappuccino, on the other hand, is espresso with richly steamed milk.

Contrary to popular opinion, the deeply roasted coffees used for espresso actually have less caffeine than lighter-roasted coffee. If caffeine is a consideration, you may also purchase decaffeinated espresso coffee. It is very important to grind the coffee to an espresso grind so that it will work properly with your espresso-making equipment.

By very lenient Italian standards, one may put a lump of sugar and a twist of lemon into espresso, but that's as far as the rules will bend. In my versions of these Italian favorites, however, we've gone beyond tradition. You'll find some espresso and cappuccino recipes which do not require a special machine, or espresso maker and are exceptionally delicious.

authentic**espresso** or **cappuccino**

- 2, 2-1/2 espresso sized cups of water (use larger amount for Cappuccino)
- 1 tablespoon finely ground espresso coffee
- ½ cup cold milk, 2% milk fat (for cappuccino)
- 2 sugar cubes (optional)
- 2 lemon twists (optional)

for this recipe, you'll need an electric or top-of-the-stove espresso maker. Later in the book, you'll see a photo of the authentic espresso maker given to me by son, Bob, during his year-long art history study in Florence, Italy. His Italian family used one like this on a daily basis.

SERVES: 2

PUT two espresso-sized cups cold water into the reservoir of an espresso machine. Lock the reservoir. Place the espresso coffee into the filter and snap the filter into place. Turn on machine. Espresso will brew in two and one-half to four minutes. Serve hot, in small cups. If desired, serve with a sugar cube or lemon twist.

FOR CAPPUCCINO: use the larger amount of water and place in reservoir. Follow the above recipe. When unit begins to brew espresso coffee, place steam nozzle of unit into the top one-half inch of the pitcher of cold milk. Allow the steam to froth and bubble the milk for a full one minute. Milk will expand to fill the pitcher and will be hot with a dry froth. Spoon froth from the milk onto the cups of espresso. Serve immediately.

Each serving (cappuccino): 46 calories; 2 gm carbohydrates; 6 gm protein; 1 gm fat (25% calories from fat); 5 mg cholesterol; 40 mg sodium; 177 mg potassium; 70 mg caffeine (made with regular coffee).

brandied**cappuccino**

- 1 cup half & half
- 2 small cups freshly-brewed espresso coffee (regular or decaf.)
- 1 tablespoon honey
- 1 tspn. cocoa (unsweetened)
- ¾ tspn. vanilla
- 2 tablespoons brandy
- 2 tablespoons Kahlua (or other coffee liqueur)
- 1 tablespoon light rum
- 1 tablespoon Galliano
- ½ cup sweetened whipped cream
- shaved chocolate

Cappuccino goes well with liqueurs. Here's a very powerful combination. If you want to reduce the alcohol and calorie content, simply boil liqueurs for about ten minutes. Add to espresso, pour into heat-proof glasses and top with whipped cream.

SERVES: 4

WHISK half and half, espresso, honey, cocoa, and vanilla in a two-quart saucepan. Heat until almost scalded. Add brandy, Kahlua, rum and Galiano and pour into four Irish whiskey (or other heat-proof wine) glasses. Garnish with whipped cream and shaved chocolate.

Each serving: 263 calories; 14 gm carbohydrates; 3 gm protein; 17 gm fat (57% calories from fat); 55 mg cholesterol; 38 mg sodium; 153 mg potassium; 36 mg caffeine (made with regular coffee); 19% calories from alcohol.

café keith

- 2 small cups freshly brewed espresso (regular or decaffeinated)
- 1 tablespoon brandy (or Grand Marnier)
- 1 tablespoon Frangelico
- ¼ cup sweetened whipped cream
- 2 cinnamon sticks (for stirring)

Thi is an adaptation from Rick's Café in Indianapolis, Indiana.

SERVES: 2

COMBINE brewed espresso with brandy and Frangelico. Pour into two large, demitasse cups. Top with whipped cream; place a cinnamon stick into each.

Each serving: 133 calories; 4 gm carbohydrate; 1 gm protein; 9 gm fat (63% calories from fat); 33 mg cholesterol; 15 mg sodium; 93 mg potassium; 70 mg caffeine (made with regular coffee); 23% calories from alcohol.

café borgatta

- 1 cup milk, 2% milk fat
- 2 tablespoons unsweetened cocoa
- 2 tablespoons granulated sugar
- 2 small cups freshly brewed espresso (regular or decaffeinated)
- ½ cup sweetened whipped cream
- grated orange

here's a rich and satisfying drink … perhaps it's the mocha of the '90s.

SERVES: 4

HEAT milk in a small saucepan. Sift cocoa and sugar into milk and whisk to blend. Stir in espresso. Divide equally into four small espresso or demitasse cups. Top with whipped cream and grated orange.

Each serving: 116 calories; 13 gm carbohydrate; 3 gm protein; 7 gm fat (48% calories from fat); 11 mg cholesterol; 50 mg sodium; 250 mg potassium; 77 mg caffeine (made with regular coffee).

café latte

- 2 cups milk, 2% milk fat
- 2 cups freshly brewed, hot espresso (regular or decaffeinated)
- ground cinnamon
- 4 cubes sugar

This is the Italian version of Cafe au Lait. In Italy, if you go to the espresso counter and stand while ordering and drinking your Cafe Latte, you'll save several thousand lira!

SERVES: 4

STEAM milk with steam nozzle of espresso maker. To froth this quantity of milk, you may also place hot milk into a blender cup and blend on highest speed for ten seconds. When milk is frothy, pour most of milk into four, warm, eight-ounce mugs. Next, pour coffee down sides of mugs. Spoon froth from milk over coffee and sprinkle with cinnamon. Serve with one cube of sugar.

Each serving: 80 calories; 9 gm carbohydrate; 5 gm protein; 2 gm fat (28% calories from fat); 10 mg cholesterol; 77 mg sodium; 291 mg potassium; 70 mg caffeine (made with regular coffee).

café latte variations

CAFE LATTE NAKED:

Serve without sugar and cinnamon

CAFE LATTE MACCHIATO:

Serve with just a dollop of foamed milk

CAFE LATTE CON PANNA:

Serve with a dollop of whipped cream

sizes

SHORT:

8 ounce cup: half espresso, half steamed milk

TALL:

12 ounce cup: 4 ounces espresso, 8 ounces steamed milk

GRANDE:

16 ounce cup: half espresso, half steamed milk

cappuccinoblanco

- ½ cup milk, 2% milk fat
- 1 vanilla bean, split
- 1 teaspoon light brown sugar
- 2 servings (6 ounces total) freshly brewed, espresso (regular or decaffeinated)
- ground cinnamon

do you like a lighter version of espresso? Maybe the espresso flavor with a little added sweetness and flavor? Then, this cappuccino is for you. It's light and sweet with a hint of vanilla.

SERVES: 2

IN a small saucepan, combine the milk and vanilla. Scald the milk. Remove from heat. Cover and let the milk steep for five minutes. Next, stir sugar into the milk. Reheat briefly and remove the vanilla bean. Transfer the milk to a blender. Whirl milk until frothy, at least forty-five seconds. Half fill two warmed, eight-ounce coffee mugs with hot espresso coffee. Add the hot milk; sprinkle with cinnamon.

Each serving: 51 calories; 6 gm carbohydrate; 2 gm protein; 1 gm fat (24% calories from fat); 5 mg cholesterol; 45 mg sodium; 255 mg potassium; 139 mg caffeine (made with regular coffee).

frosty minted**mocha**

- 2 tablespoons chocolate syrup
- 2 small cups freshly brewed espresso coffee (regular or decaffeinated)
- 2 ounces milk, 2% milk fat
- 1 teaspoon mint extract
- crushed ice
- 2 mint leaves

This light, tasty espresso is the perfect ending to dinner on a hot night. It's easy to prepare, and you may use hot or cold espresso.

SERVES: 2

IN a blender, combine chocolate syrup, coffee, milk, mint extract, and crushed ice. Blend until frothy. Pour into a ten-ounce glass and garnish with a mint leaf.

Each serving: 65 calories; 13 gm carbohydrate; 1 gm protein; 1 gm fat (10% calories form fat); 1 mg cholesterol; 35 mg sodium; 240 mg potassium; 141 mg caffeine (made with regular coffee).

iced elegantissimo

- 2 small cups freshly brewed espresso (regular or decaffeinated)
- ½ cup superfine granulated sugar
- 1 square (1 ounce) semi-sweet chocolate, chopped
- 2 cups finely crushed ice
- ¼ cup heavy cream
- chocolate shavings for garnish

This is the ultimate. Make it in advance, then watch as your guests rave over this sweet, chocolate delight. It's worth every one of its calories.

SERVES: 4

STIR the hot espresso, sugar, and chocolate together until the sugar dissolves and the chocolate melts. Refrigerate until well chilled, three hours or overnight.

FILL wine glasses with finely crushed ice. Pour the cold coffee over the ice. Whisk the cream until just thick enough to mount onto a spoon. Place a spoonful on each glass. Top with chocolate shavings and serve with a straw.

Each serving: 180 calories; 29 gm carbohydrate; 1 gm protein; 8 gm fat (38% calories from fat); 20 mg cholesterol; 10 mg sodium; 102 mg potassium; 74 mg caffeine (made with regular coffee).

microwave
cappuccino

- 1 cup vanilla ice cream
- 4 microwave-proof wine glasses (or Irish coffee glasses), 8 ounces each
- 4 cups Italian Espresso Coffee (regular or decaffeinated) brewed in a regular coffee maker (use a paper filter)

This faux recipe is fun. It is also quick, delicious, and has quite the authentic flavor. It was given to me by my friend, Lila Greenberg, who lives in the San Francisco Bay Area.

SERVES: 4

SCOOP one-fourth cup ice cream into each glass. Microwave until ice cream is warm and bubbled up into the cup, one and one-half to two minutes (for all four glasses). Add brewed espresso.

Each serving: 95 calories; 9 gm carbohydrate; 1 gm protein; 6 gm fat (58% calories from fat); 22 mg cholesterol; 35 mg sodium; 191 mg potassium; 139 mg caffeine (made with regular coffee).

mocha fino

- 2 small cups freshly-brewed espresso (regular or decaffeinated)
- 2 teaspoons sugar
- 1 teaspoon unsweetened cocoa powder
- 1 cup half and half
- shaved chocolate

here's a mocha with a subtle, espresso flavor...it's a dream!

SERVES: 2

INTO two, ten-ounce mugs, pour espresso, sugar and cocoa powder. Heat cream; divide between two mugs. Sprinkle with chocolate shavings.

Each serving: 267 calories; 10 gm carbohydrate; 3 gm protein; 24 gm fat (80% calories from fat; 80 mg cholesterol; 56 mg sodium; 297 mg potassium; 141 mg caffeine (made with regular coffee).

The Opera Event

After the Opera, what could be more blissful than spirited coffee and confections?

PHOTO CREDITS

Opera glasses, courtesy of Johnson's Optical, Cleveland, Ohio; opera gloves, Westlake Resale, Cleveland, Ohio; crystal coffee set from Antiques in the Bank, Cleveland, Ohio; lace tablecloth from Dillard's; gold serving plate courtesy of Mary Ward; silver teaspoon courtesy of Al's Pottery.

RECIPE CREDITS

Regular or decaf coffee served with Coffee Liqueur, page 170
Olliebollen, page 182

COFFEE WITH SPIRITS

Coffee makes a great ending to a meal. And the recipes in this chapter will enhance and enchant your guests. Whether it's an intimate party for two or a dinner party for twelve, your guests will enjoy coffee with spirits.

You'll notice we've added a new figure to the nutrition analysis for this chapter: percentage of calories from alcohol. These recipes are delicious and different. So, if you don't need to count calories, enjoy.

If you are like some of us, though, you'll want to know how many calories you are consuming with that dessert cup of coffee. One of the easiest ways to reduce the calories in any of these spirited recipes is to boil the alcohol before adding to the coffee. In this way, you'll remove almost all of the alcohol and with it the calories.

In addition, you may want to use decaffeinated coffee for these recipes. If you do plan to use decaf, I would suggest you start with a decaffeinated Colombia Supremo, then add French roast decaf, and espresso decaf to your collection.

So, here's to the spirit of coffee drinking while drinking coffee with spirits!

black**beauty**

- 1 ounce brandy
- 1 ounce dark rum, 100 proof
- 4 ounces black coffee (regular or decaffeinated)
- 2 teaspoons powdered sugar

a recipe for brandy lovers!

SERVES: 1

PLACE cracked ice into a large, heat-proof brandy snifter. Pour ingredients over and stir.

Each serving: 171 calories; 5 gm carbohydrates; 0 protein; 0 gm fat; 0 cholesterol; 4 mg sodium; 136 mg potassium; 64 mg caffeine (made with regular coffee); 89% calories from alcohol.

brandied**coffee**punch

- 6 eggs
- grated peel of one lemon
- ½ cup granulted sugar
- 3 cups cold, strong coffee (regular or decaffeinated)
- 2/3 cup brandy or cognac

This is a holiday punch, served at Christmas in Denmark. My recipe comes to me via New Orleans and Phyllis Jordan's PJ's Coffee & Tea Co., Inc. This is sweet, creamy, delicious.

SERVES: 6

BEAT eggs and lemon peel until mixture is light and fluffy. Add sugar a little at a time, beating continuously. Continue beating until thick. Slowly stir in the coffee and then add brandy or cognac.

SERVE IN CHILLED GLASSES.

Each serving: 211 calories; 17 gm carbohydrate; 6 gm protein; 6 gm fat (24% calories from fat); 274 mg cholesterol; 73 mg sodium; 133 mg potassium, 70 mg caffeine (made with regular coffee); 33 % calories from alcohol.

brandy**frosted**

- 2 tablespoons granulated sugar
- 4 ice cubes
- 1 cup cold, strong, black coffee (regular or decaffeinated)
- 1 cup half and half
- 2 ounces brandy (or Grand Marnier)
- ¼ cup sweetened whipped cream

The flavors of brandy and coffee here are subtly blended with the richness of cream. This coffee is delicious with or without brandy.

SERVES: 2

IN blender cup, place sugar, ice cubes, and coffee. Blend for twenty seconds on medium. Remove cap and add half and half and brandy. Blend for five seconds. Pour iced coffee into two, tall glasses. Top with sweetened whipped cream.

Each serving: 456 calories; 24 gm carbohydrate; 7 gm protein; 29 mg fat (58% calories from fat); 95 mg cholesterol; 115 mg sodium; 461 mg potassium; 139 mg caffeine (made with regular coffee);15% calories from alcohol.

cafe **au** vin

- 1 cup cold strong French roast coffee (regular or decaffeinated)
- 2 ounces Tawny Port
- 2 tablespoons granulated sugar
- ½ teaspoon grated orange peel
- dash of cinnamon

You don't often think of serving coffee with wine. Tawny port has the body and flavor to make a nice marriage with French roast coffee. We think you'll appreciate this as a great dinner coffee.

SERVES: 2

COMBINE ingredients and mix in a blender cup at high speed. Pour into chilled wine glasses.

Each serving: 94 calories; 16 gm carbohydrate; 0 protein; 0 gm fat; 0 cholesterol; 5 mg sodium; 89 mg potassium; 70 mg caffeine (made with regular coffee); 31% calories from alcohol.

café flambe

- 2 sugar cubes
- 2 teaspoons brandy or cognac
- 2 cups hot coffee (regular or decaffeinated)

This is a dramatic, yet simple and fun idea-recipe.

SERVES: 2

SOAK a cube of sugar in brandy for ten minutes. Place into a teaspoon and hold so that it will rest on top of the cup of coffee. Ignite. Hold until flame burns out and drop contents into the coffee.

Each serving: 12 calories; 3 gm carbohydrate; 0 protein; 0 fat (no calories from fat); 0 cholesterol; 8 mg sodium; 139 mg caffeine (made with regular coffee); no calories from alcohol as it has burned out!

café jamaica

- 2 ounces Kahlua (or coffee liqueur)
- 2 ounces dark rum, 100 proof
- 2 cups strong, hot coffee (regular or decaffeinated)
- ¼ cup sweetened whipped cream
- nutmeg (for garnish)

here's a great hot coffee with a tropical twist. It's also great when poured over crushed ice.

SERVES: 2

PLACE Kahlua and rum into two, heat-proof coffee mugs. Add coffee. Stir. Top with whipped cream and nutmeg.

Each serving: 270 calories; 13 gm carbohydrate; 1 gm protein; 9 gm fat (31% calories from fat); 33 mg cholesterol; 15 mg sodium; 94 mg potassium; 69 mg caffeine (made with regular coffee); 49% calories from alcohol.

campfire**café**

- 1 orange
- 1 lemon
- 16 cloves
- 1 quart plus 1 cup very cold water
- 6 tablespoons French Market Coffee (coffee with chicory)
- 8 sugar cubes
- 8 cinnamon pieces, 1 inch each
- 8 ounces brandy or cognac

here's a recipe from a good friend in Dallas, Texas, Ron Weunsch. Ron is an avid hunter who likes a warm campfire, close friends, and a Campfire Cafe on a brisk fall evening.

SERVES: 6

PEEL orange into one, long peel. Do the same with lemon. Stud each long peel with cloves (eight each). Over campfire, heat water in a large, open pan. When water is boiling, add coffee and allow to boil for five minutes. When time is up, add one more cup cold water to settle out grounds.

IN second pan, heat studded orange and lemon peels, sugar cubes, and cinnamon pieces until sugar melts. Add strained, hot coffee to mixture. Slightly warm cognac or brandy.

IGNITE. Holding orange and lemon peels with heat-proof tongs, slowly pour burning brandy down peels into hot coffee. Strain again and serve in large mugs.

Each serving: 18 calories; 3 carbohydrates; 0 protein; 0 gm fat; 0 cholesterol; 8 mg sodium; 136 mg potassium; 139 mg caffeine (made with regular coffee); no calories from alcohol as it is burned out.

café seville

- ½ cup chopped ice
- 2 cups strong, cold coffee (regular or decaffeinated)
- 2 tablespoons granulated sugar
- ¼ cup Cointreau
- ¼ teaspoon grated orange peel
- 1 cup milk, 2% milk fat
- 2 slices orange

This is a refreshing beverage to serve with salads or desserts. It is frothy, with just a tang from citrus and Cointreau.

SERVES: 2

PLACE all ingredients except orange slices into a blender cup and blend at a high speed until frothy. Divide between two, sixteen-ounce glasses. Garnish with orange slices.

Each serving: 229 calories; 32 gm carbohydrate; 5 gm protein; 2 gm fat (9% calories from fat); 10 mg cholesterol; 81 mg sodium; 400 mg potassium; 139 mg caffeine (made with regular coffee); 28% calories from alcohol.

chocolate
grasshopper

- 1 cup strong, cold coffee (regular or decaffeinated)
- 1 cup chocolate ice cream
- 2 ounces white creme de menthe
- 4 mint sprigs for garnish

here's a lovely dessert coffee. Serve it in wide-mouthed champagne glasses with a straw and pizzelle cookies.

SERVES: 4

MIX all ingredients in blender cup. Blend at low speed. Pour into four, wide-mouthed champagne or wine glasses. Garnish with mint sprig.

Each serving: 141 calories; 14 gm carbohydrate; 1 gm protein; 6 gm fat (37% calories from fat); 22 mg cholesterol; 30 mg sodium; 89 mg potassium; 35 mg caffeine (made with regular coffee); 21 % calories from alcohol.

danish**coffee**

- 2 small demitasse cups
- 2 ounces hot, strong coffee (regular or decaffeinated)
- 2 ounces aquavit or kummel (caraway liqueur)

here's an interesting way to clarify your coffee.

SERVES: 2

PLACE a clean dime in the bottom of both coffee cups. Cover with coffee until it is no longer visible. Now, pour liqueur into the cup until the coin appears again. (Don't drink the dime!)

Each serving: 170 calories; 1 gm carbohydrate; 0 protein; 0 gm fat; 0 cholesterol; 8 mg sodium; 136 mg potassium; 139 mg caffeine (made with regular coffee); 97% calories from alcohol.

devil's**delight**

- **2 cups freshly brewed French roast coffee (regular or decaffeinated)**
- **4 tablespoons Kahlua (or coffee liqueur)**
- **1 tablespoon creme de cacao**
- **1 cup whipping cream, whipped**
- **4 tablespoonfuls chocolate syrup**

devilishly rich…with more than a hint of Kahlua.

SERVES: 4

BLEND together coffee, Kahlua, and creme de cacao. Pour into four, heat-proof parfait glasses, eight ounces each. Top each with one-fourth cup whipped cream. Dot with chocolate syrup dots to resemble chocolate chips.

Each serving: 285 calories; 12 gm carbohydrate; 1 gm protein; 22 gm fat (68% calories from fat); 82 mg cholesterol; 30 mg sodium; 130 mg potassium; 70 mg caffeine (made with regular coffee); 14% calories from alcohol.

irish**coffee**

- ½ pint whipping cream
- 2 tablespoons granulated sugar
- 1 teaspoon vanilla extract
- 6 ounces Irish whiskey
- 6 tablespoons brown sugar
- 6 cups freshly brewed French roast coffee (regular or decaffeinated)

The traditional recipe.

SERVES: 6

IN a chilled bowl, beat whipping cream with sugar and vanilla until firm. In six Irish whiskey glasses (or eight-ounce, heat-proof wine glasses), pour one ounce Irish whisky, a tablespoon of brown sugar and coffee. Stir. Gently place whipped cream on coffee. Serve immediately.

Each serving: 281 calories; 19 gm carbohydrate; 1 gm protein; 15 gm fat (41% calories from fat); 54 mg cholesterol; 27 mg sodium; 213 mg potassium; 139 mg caffeine (made with regular coffee); 33% calories from alcohol.

irish**coffee**(NO LIQUOR)

- 1 cup strong, hot coffee (regular or decaffeinated)
- 1 tablespoon orange juice
- 1 teaspoon lemon juice
- 2 tablespoons sweetened whipped cream

This has the authentic Irish coffee flavor…without the alcohol!

SERVES: 1

POUR hot coffee into an eight-ounce, heat-proof wine glass or Irish whiskey glass. Add orange juice and lemon juice. Stir. Top with whipped cream.

Each serving: 35 calories; 4 gm carbohydrate; 0 protein; 2 gm fat (48% calories from fat); 6 mg cholesterol; 18 mg sodium; 184 mg potassium; 139 mg caffeine (made with regular coffee).

italian**coffee**

- 3 ounces Amaretto liqueur
- 2 cups Italian roast coffee (regular or decaffeinated)
- 1 scoop coffee ice cream
- ground coriander

This unusual recipe is an innovative way to complete an Italian meal. It is light and satisfying.

SERVES: 2

DIVIDE Amaretto into two, heat-resistance wine glasses or mugs. Fill with coffee. Top each coffee with one-half scoop of ice cream and a sprinkle of coriander.

Each serving: 231 calories; 22 gm carbohydrate; 1 gm protein; 6 gm fat (23% calories from fat); 22 mg cholesterol; 35 mg sodium; 219 mg potassium; 139 mg caffeine; 38% calories from alcohol.

italian**coffee II**

- ■ 1 pint whipping cream
- ■ 2 ounces Galliano (or Neopolitan liqueur)
- ■ 4 cups French or Italian roast coffee (regular or decaffeinated)

another great, rich Italian coffee!

SERVES: 4

WHIP cream with liqueur until firm. Pour coffee into four, heat-proof wine glasses. Top with whipped cream.

Each serving: 258 calories; 7 gm carbohydrate; 1 gm protein; 22 gm fat (76% calories from fat); 82 mg cholesterol; 30 mg sodium; 180 mg potassium; 139 mg caffeine (made with regular coffee); 11% calories from alcohol.

italiancoffee III

- 2 ounces Amaretto liqueur
- 2 ounces dark rum
- 4 cups strong, hot coffee (regular or decaffeinated)
- 4 tablespoons heavy cream

another twist on Italian coffee.

SERVES: 4

BLEND Amaretto and rum; divide between four, heat-proof wine glasses. Pour in coffee. Stir. Float heavy cream on top.

Each serving: 150 calories; 6 gm carbohydrate; 0 protein; 6 gm fat (29% calories from fat); 20 mg cholesterol; 14 mg sodium; 147 mg potassium; 139 mg caffeine (made with regular coffee); 56% calories from alcohol.

mexican**coffee**

- 2 ounces Kahlua (or coffee liqueur)
- 1 ounce Tequila
- 2 cups strong, hot coffee (preferably Mexican Coffee)
- ¼ cup whipped cream
- ground cinnamon

mexican food is great at Luchita's in Cleveland with wonderful Mexican coffee. Here is an adaptation of their recipe.

SERVES: 2

POUR Kahlua and tequila into a coffee mug. Add coffee. Stir. Top with whipped cream and cinnamon.

Each serving: 233 calories; 24 gm carbohydrate; 1 gm protein; 9 gm fat (36% calories from fat); 33 mg cholesterol; 19 mg sodium; 158 mg potassium; 140 mg caffeine (made with regular coffee); 40% calories from alcohol.

mocha**rum**punch

- 1 cup whipping cream
- 1 tablespoon granulated sugar
- 1 teaspoon pure vanilla extract
- 1 pint chocolate ice cream, cut into 2-inch chunks
- ¼ cup dark rum (more, if desired)
- 4 cups freshly brewed coffee (regular or decaffeinated)

anna Turner Mysenbery is a food editor in South Florida. She writes that this recipe is a "southern party fare."

SERVES: 12

WHIP cream with sugar and vanilla until it is firm. Blend in ice cream. Combine with coffee and rum. Pour into a twelve-cup punch bowl. Stir until smooth. Serve immediately.

Each serving: 146 calories; 7 gm carbohydrate; 1 gm protein; 11 gm fat (65% calories from fat); 42 mg cholesterol; 28 mg sodium; 97 mg potassium; 46 mg caffeine (made with regular coffee); 13% calories from alcohol.

spiced**coffee**bracer

- **2 cups cold, strong coffee (regular or decaffeinated)**
- **2 ounces light rum**
- **2 tablespoons granulated sugar**
- **2 tablespoons light cream**
- **dash powdered cloves**
- **dash allspice**
- **2 cinnamon sticks**

Be sure to try this great cocktail coffee. It's spicy, refreshing, and light.

SERVES: 2

FILL two twelve-ounce tall drink glasses with ice cubes. Add coffee, rum, sugar, cream, cloves, and allspice. Stir. Garnish with cinnamon sticks.

Each serving: 107 calories; 5 gm carbohydrate; 1 gm protein; 2 gm fat (15% calories from fat); 6 mg cholesterol; 14 mg sodium; 155 mg potassium; 139 mg caffeine (made with regular coffee); 63% calories from alcohol.

iced**creme**de**cacao**

- 2 cups strong, cold coffee
- 2 teaspoons simple syrup (page 114)
- 2 ounces creme de cacao
- 2 tablespoons whipped cream, whipped
- ½ teaspoon cocoa powder
- ½ teaspoon grated orange peel

This is an ideal ending to a cool, summer meal.

SERVES: 2

BLEND coffee with syrup and creme de cacao. Pour into two, ten-ounce stemmed glasses. Top with whipped cream, cocoa, and orange peel.

Each serving: 189 calories; 18 gm carbohydrate; trace protein; 5 gm fat (25% calories from fat); 17 mg cholesterol; 15 mg sodium; 150 mg potassium; 140 mg caffeine (made with regular coffee).

coffeeliqueur

- 1, 2-inch vanilla bean
- 1 cup cold water
- 1 cup dark roast coffee
- 1 cup vodka
- ¾ cup brown sugar
- ¼ cup white sugar
- 2 tablespoons dark molasses (optional)

here's a delicious, homemade version of Kahlua. Although not as heavy as the commercial variety, our coffee liqueur is light and flavorful. For a heavier coffee liqueur, add dark molasses.

SERVES: 16, 1-OUNCE SERVINGS

PLACE vanilla bean in coffee carafe. Brew coffee according to manufacturers' directions. (If coffee grounds will not fit in your filter basket, brew twice using half the coffee each time.) Allow coffee to cool. Brew through the grounds a second time.* Immediately add vodka, sugars and optional molasses. Pour into a clean, quart bottle with a tight-fitting stopper. Allow to cure for two days, then serve as Kahlua.

Each serving: 84 calories;11 gm carbohydrate; 0 gm protein; 0 gm fat (no calories from fat); 0 mg cholesterol; 12 mg sodium; 164 mg potassium; 140 mg caffeine (made with regular coffee); 46% calories from alcohol.

* After brewing coffee through the coffee maker, cool machine. Then clean as directed on page 37.

Coffee on a Picnic

Delicious coffee can go anywhere when an insulated pitcher is used.

PHOTO CREDITS

Picnic basket courtesy of Mary Ward; plastic dinnerware from Dillard's; bandana from K Mart; insulated pitcher from Thermos.

RECIPE CREDITS

Toffee Coffee, page 88

Amaretto Coffee Cheesecake, Page 174

For this presentation, the cheesecake was cooled completely, then topped with 2 cups prepared cherry pie filling.

COFFEE BREAK RECIPES

Coffee break is an American tradition. So, the foods served at coffee break should be truly American. Look at this collection of recipes: a Kona cookie from Hawaii, A Cinnamon Toast Coffee Cake from the Yukon, a New York Style Amaretto Cheesecake from New York City, an elegant Charlotte from Texas, everyone's favorite Chocolate Cake from Florida, and…you can't top this…a Banana Split Frozen Dessert from Silicon Valley. These recipes will be sure to spark conversation and conviviality at your next coffee break.

You'll notice from the calorie and fat analysis that many of these recipes are calorie and fat consuming. Any recipe may be adapted for low fat and cholesterol diets by doing the following: substitute half of the margarine or butter with corn syrup; use only the white of the egg (substituting 2 egg whites for each egg); use low-fat or non-fat cream cheese, sour cream, ricotta, milk, chocolate morsels and cheese. To reduce sugar, you may subtract up to 1/3 of the sugar required for each recipe. Use ½ less salt, if desired. Alcohol is optional in any recipe and decaf coffee may be substituted for regular coffee. So…here's to your next Coffee Break!

amaretto**coffee** cheesecake

- 1 tablespoon butter
- ½ cup graham cracker crumbs
- 1 container, 16 ounces, ricotta cheese
- 2 packages, 8 ounces each, cream cheese, room temperature
- 2 cups buttermilk
- 1-1/2 cups sugar, divided
- 6 eggs, separated
- 2 tablespoons lemon zest
- 1-1/2 cups all purpose flour
- 2 tablespoons Amaretto liquer
- 2 tablespoons strong, cold coffee or espresso
- ½ cup heavy cream, whipped
- confectioners sugar

here's a New York style cheesecake—it's creamy, light with just a spark of Amaretto. It serves 16, and it's worth every calorie and gram of fat.

SERVES: 16

PREHEAT oven to 425 degrees F. Generously butter a 10-inch spring form pan. Sprinkle bottom of pan with graham cracker crumbs. In a large bowl, place ricotta, cream cheese and buttermilk. Gradually beat in 1 cup sugar and egg yolks. Beat after each addition of egg yolk. Stir in lemon zest, flour, Amaretto, and espresso. In a medium-sized bowl, whip egg whites until frothy. Sprinkle remaining sugar, a tablespoon at a time, over the egg whites.

BEAT until egg whites hold peaks. Fold in whipped cream, then fold into the cheese mixture. Turn into prepared spring form pan. Smooth top.

BAKE for 10 minutes at 425 degrees F. Lower oven to 350 degrees F. and bake 1 hour longer. Turn oven heat off and allow cake to cool with the door closed. (This will prevent formation of large cracks in the surface.)

WHEN cooled completely, cover and store in the refrigerator. Sprinkle with confectioners sugar to serve.

Each serving: 355 calories; 36 gm carbohydrate; 11 gm protein; 10 gm fat (47% of calories from fat); 156 mg cholesterol; 222 mg sodium; 186 mg potassium.

chocolate**chip**loaf

- non-stick cooking spray
- 2 cups all purpose flour
- ¾ cup brown sugar, packed
- 3 teaspoons baking powder
- 1 teaspoon salt
- 1 tablespoon lemon zest
- 1 cup walnuts or pecans, chopped
- 1 package, 6 ounces, semi-sweet chocolate morsels
- 1 egg
- 1 cup applesauce
- 2 tablespoons vegetable oil

COFFEE GLAZE
- 1-1/2 cups confectioners sugar, sifted
- 2 teaspoons cool coffee
- 3 tablespoons brandy

...CHOCOLATE CHIP COOKIE TASTE...with the convenience of baking in a loaf pan. This loaf cake has an irresistible topping. The recipe is the favorite coffee break treat of an art director in Columbus, Ohio.

SERVES: 10

PREHEAT over to 350 degrees F. Spray a 9x5x3 inch loaf pan with non-stick cooking spray. In a medium sized mixing bowl, blend flour with brown sugar, baking powder and salt. Add lemon zest, nuts and chocolate morsels.

BEAT egg with applesauce and oil. Add to the flour mixture, stirring until just blended. Pour into prepared pan.

BAKE for 1 hour. While loaf is baking, mix confectioners sugar with coffee and brandy. Allow baked loaf to cool for 10 minutes before removing from pan.

GLAZE with Coffee Glaze while loaf is still hot. Cool, then wrap and store for 8 hours or overnight before slicing.

Each serving using brandy in the glaze: 307 calories; 44 gm carbohydrates; 7 gm protein; 11 gm fat (32% calories from fat); 29 cholesterol; 320 mg sodium; 299 mg potassium.

cinnamon**toast** **coffee**cake

- non-stick cooking spray
- 1 cup sugar
- 2 teaspoons butter
- 1 teaspoon salt
- 2 cups all-purpose flour
- 1 teaspoon baking powder
- 1 cup milk
- 1 teaspoon vanilla
- 4 tablespoons melted butter
- 1 tablespoon cinnamon
- ½ cup sugar

If you're looking for a great tasting coffee cake then consider this recipe! It's light and full of flavor…it was given to me by a coffee shop owner from the Yukon. She says, "Eat it hot and eat a lot."

SERVES: 8

PREHEAT oven to 325 degrees F. Spray a 9x13x4 inch baking pan with non-stick cooking spray. In a large mixing bowl, blend together sugar, butter, and salt. In a medium-sized mixing bowl, sift flour with baking powder. Add flour mixture to the sugar mixture.

STIR in the milk and vanilla and blend well. Pour into prepared pan and bake for 15-20 minutes or until the top is golden brown.

DRIZZLE melted butter over the top of the coffee cake. In a small bowl, mix cinnamon and remaining sugar. Sprinkle over the top of the coffee cake.

RETURN the cake to the oven and bake for 10 minutes longer. Serve hot!

Each serving: 348 calories; 63 gm carbohydrate; 5 gm protein; 9 gm fat (24% calories from fat); 25 mg cholesterol; 439 mg sodium; 136 mg potassium.

coffee**honey**bread

- non-stick cooking spray
- 1/3 cup warm water
- 5 tablespoons honey
- 5 tablespoons light margarine, melted
- 2 packages, ¼ ounce each, yeast
- 5 cups all-purpose flour or a mixture of all-purpose and whole wheat or oat bran flour
- ½ teaspoon salt
- 6 tablespoons milk, scalded
- 4 egg whites
- 3 tablespoons coffee, cooled
- ¼ cup pistachio nuts, finely chopped

here's a bread that is as nutritious as it is delicious. Make it with part whole wheat or oat bran flour for even more nutrition. It comes from a Chicago coffee lovers' kitchen. Even better, it makes 2 loaves.

SERVES: 32

SPRAY 2, 9x5x3 inch baking pans with non-stick cooking spray. Set aside. In a small bowl, blend water with honey, margarine, and yeast. Allow this mixture to stand for 5 minutes until the yeast is bubbly. In a large mixing bowl or food processor bowl fitted with a dough hook, mix flour and salt.

BLEND in hot milk, egg whites, yeast mixture, and coffee. Blend until mixture cleans the sides of the mixing bowl or food processor. Mix in pistachios.

PLACE dough in a large, well-oiled mixing bowl. Cover and place in a warm location away from drafts. Allow bread to rise until doubled in size, about 45 minutes.

PREHEAT over to 375 degrees F. Divide dough between pans, smooth tops. Bake for 35-40 minutes.

REMOVE from pans onto a cooling rack while still warm. Cool before slicing.

Each serving: 100 calories; 18 gm carbohydrates; 4 gm protein; 2 gm fat (15% calories from fat); less than 1 mg cholesterol; 61 mg sodium; 112 mg potassium.

dutch**doughnuts**
(OLLIEBOLLEN)

- 1 cake yeast, 2/3 ounce
- 1 cup milk
- 1-1/4 cups all purpose flour
- 1 teaspoon salt
- 1 egg
- 1-1/2 cup raisins
- 1 tart cooking apple (such as Granny Smith), peeled and minced
- 2-4 quarts vegetable oil for deep frying
- 1 cup confectioners sugar

While in Groningen, Holland, one year, I visited the market plaza. In this centuries' old plaza, I was able to sample a traditional treat, "Olliebollen", or Dutch Style Doughnuts. They are perfect with coffee.

SERVES: 30

CRUMBLE yeast into a medium-sized mixing bowl. Heat milk to warm and pour over yeast. Allow to rest for 5 minutes. Sift flour and salt into the yeast mixture, then stir in the egg and sugar. Mix until smooth.

ADD the raisins and apple. Allow the batter to rise in a warm place for 30 minutes. It should double its size.

HEAT oil in a heavy pan or deep fat fryer. The heat should be 375 degrees F. or hot enough to fry a small piece of bread golden brown in a minute. With 2 large spoons, shape doughnuts into golf ball-sized pieces and drop them, 1 at a time, carefully into the hot fat. The doughnuts should be evenly browned in 4-5 minutes.

DRAIN onto paper towels. While still warm, sift a thick coating of confectioners sugar onto the doughnuts.

Each serving: 102 calories; 16 gm carbohydrates; 2 gm protein; 4 gm fat (34% calories from fat); 10 mg cholesterol; 74 mg sodium; 98 mg potassium.

eggless**buttermilk** **coffee**cake

- non-stick cooking spray
- 2 cups brown sugar, packed
- 2 cups all-purpose flour
- ½ cup butter
- 1 teaspoon baking soda
- ½ teaspoon salt
- 1 cup buttermilk or sour milk

at Coffee Tea and Spice Coffee Shop in the Yukon, the customer is King! The proprietor has on-going classes in coffee brewing. I suspect that customers do a fair amount of coffee consumption during those long, cold Whitehorse, Yukon, winters. Here's the proprietor's answer to a great coffee cake. This coffee cake freezes well and may be "rejuvenated" by heating, covered, for 10 minutes in a 350 degree F oven.

SERVES: 9

PREHEAT oven to 350 degrees F. Spray a 9x9x2 inch square baking pan with non-stick cooking spray. In a medium-sized mixing bowl, mix the sugar, flour, and butter until it has the consistency of fine crumbs.

REMOVE and reserve ½ cup of the mixture for the topping. To the remaining flour mixture, add baking soda, salt and buttermilk. Blend well. Spread into prepared pan.

SPRINKLE the reserved crumbs over the top of the cake.

BAKE for 30 minutes or until a toothpick inserted into the center comes out clean. Watch carefully as the brown sugar topping burns easily.

Each serving: 383 calories; 70 gm carbohydrates; 4 gm protein;1 gm fat (24% calories from fat); 28 mg cholesterol; 348 mg sodium; 239 mg potassium.

frozen**banana** **split**dessert

- 3 cups graham cracker crumbs
- 2/3 cup melted butter
- 6 tablespoons sugar
- 3 bananas, sliced
- ½ gallon coffee ice cream, softened
- 1 cup walnuts, chopped
- ½ cup butter
- 1 cup chocolate morsels
- 2 cups confectioners sugar
- 1-1/2 cups evaporated milk
- 1 teaspoon vanilla
- 1 pint vanilla ice cream, softened
- 1 pint whipping cream
- 2 tablespoons confectioners sugar
- 1 teaspoon vanilla

This recipe originates in San Jose, California, where it was submitted to me by a news reporter. About the dessert, he says, "...a lot of work, but well worth the effort. Superior!" I agree, it's wonderful. Note: This will store or travel well when placed in a styrofoam cooler with 3 pounds of dry ice. It can be successfully made with non-fat products.

SERVES: 36

MIX together graham cracker crumbs, butter and 6 tablespoons sugar. Reserve 1 cup of this mixture. Place the remainder in the bottom of a 10x14 inch decorative dish.

PLACE bananas atop crumbs. Next, place softened ice cream atop bananas. Layer walnuts and freeze until firm, about 2 hours. Place, butter, chocolate morsels, 2 cups confectioners sugar, and evaporated milk in a heavy pan and heat until chips melt and sugar is dissolved. Add vanilla. Cool slightly, then pour over frozen mixture.

SPREAD softened ice cream atop and freeze overnight (or at least 8 hours). Whip cream with 2 tablespoons confectioners sugar and vanilla until it forms stiff peaks.

SPREAD over ice cream layer and top with reserved crumbs. Freeze another 2 hours...then serve with plenty of hot coffee.

Each serving: 305 calories; 29 gm carbohydrates; 4 gm. protein; 20 gm fat (59% calories from fat); 51 mg cholesterol; 146 mg sodium; 200 mg potassium.

hazelnut**creme** **coffee**charlotte

- ½ cup water
- ½ cup plus 2 tablespoons sugar
- ¾ cup Hazelnut Cream flavored coffee beans, cracked*
- 1-1/2 quarts milk
- 12 egg yolks
- 1-1/2 cups confectioners sugar
- ¼ ounce package gelatin powder
- 1 tablespoon Frangelico liqueur
- 12 lady fingers, split
- 1 cup heavy whipping cream
- ¼ cup confectioners sugar
- ½ cup sweetened whipped cream (for garnish)

*TO CRACK COFFEE BEANS: place in clear plastic storage bag and tap gently with hammer. Each bean should crack into 4 or 5 pieces.

This recipe comes from The Coffee Company in Dallas. It's their version of one created by the chef at Cleo. It takes time…but it's delicious!

SERVES: 24

MAKE a simple syrup by boiling water and ½ cup plus 2 tablespoons sugar in a small saucepan. Boil together until well-blended. Cool and set aside.

ADD cracked coffee beans to 1 quart milk and bring to a boil in a medium-sized saucepan. Allow this mixture to infuse for 30 minutes over low heat. In a large mixing bowl, beat egg yolks and 1-1/2 cups confectioners sugar until the mixture becomes thick and creamy.

WHISK remaining milk into the egg yolk-sugar mixture.

POUR this mixture into a heavy, 4 quart saucepan and stir slowly over low heat with a wooden spoon.

CONTINUE to stir until the mixture becomes creamy. It will be hot, but do not let it boil!

STRAIN hot coffee-milk through a fine mesh strainer stirring with a metal spoon to help the coffee-milk through the strainer. Set aside 2 cups of the coffee-milk for use in the final presentation of the Charlotte.

NEXT, dissolve the gelatin powder with 3 tablespoons of water. Add to the remainder of the coffee-milk. Let this cool, but do not chill.

ADD Frangelico and egg mixture and stir well.

TO PREPARE THE CHARLOTTE PAN: roll each lady finger in simple syrup one at a time and place around the sides of a 6" wide by 5" deep charlotte pan (a 9" tube pan will also work).

PLACE any remaining lady fingers in the bottom of the pan. Whip the cup of whipping cream with ¼ cup confectioners sugar until stiff, then fold into the coffee-gelatin-egg mixture.

POUR the mixture into the charlotte pan and place in the refrigerator for 6 hours or overnight.

TO SERVE: loosen the edges of the charlotte; carefully; remove the charlotte onto a round serving platter or try. Garnish the edges with additional sweetened whipped cream. Spoon the reserved coffee crème onto 24 dessert plates.

DIVIDE the charlotte among the plates.

Each serving: 240 calories; 28 gm carbohydrates; 5 gm protein; 12 gm fat (45% calories from fat); 135 mg cholesterol; 70 mg sodium; 150 mg potassium; 6 mg caffeine.

kahlua**cheese**muffins

- 1 box, 18 to 20 ounces, chocolate cake mix
- 1/3 cup pecans, chopped
- 1/3 cup butter, melted
- 1 package, 8 ounces, cream cheese
- 2 tablespoons sugar
- ¼ cup Kahlua or coffee liqueur
- 3 tablespoons freshly brewed, strong coffee
- 1 egg
- ¾ cup half and half

This recipe comes from a friend in McKinney, Texas. She is a home economist and an excellent cook. When she isn't teaching cooking....she cooks for family and friends. She's used and improved on this recipe for many years. Made in mini-muffin pans, it makes great holiday gifts.

SERVES: 48

GREASE 48 mini muffin pans (or use mini paper liners). Preheat oven to 300 degrees F. Reserve 1 cup cake mix.

COMBINE remaining cake mix in a large bowl with pecans and butter.

BLEND with pastry blender or dough hook until the mixture is blended and crumbly. Press onto the bottom and sides of mini muffin tins.

IN a medium-sized bowl, beat cream cheese, sugar, Kahlua, and coffee.

BEAT in reserved cake mix. Add egg and blend well. Gradually add in half and half. Divide cream cheese mixture among the crusts. Bake for 45 to 55 minutes.

CHILL well before serving so that the crust has a chance to "set up."

Each serving: 90 calories; 7 gm carbohydrate; 4 gm protein; 6 gm fat (60% calories from fat); 16 mg cholesterol; 78 mg sodium; 34 mg potassium.

keljner

- 1 egg
- 1 egg yolk
- 1/3 cup sugar
- ¼ cup butter, melted
- ¼ cup light cream
- ½ teaspoon baking powder
- 1-1/2 – cups all purpose flour
- 2-4 quarts vegetable oil for deep fat frying
- ½ cup confectioners sugar

This is a light delicacy…somewhat like a sweet pie crust. A Norwegian treat, it is great served with steaming mugs of coffee. These little bowl shaped pastries will be the favorite at every Coffee Klatch.

SERVES: 24

IN a large mixing bowl, beat egg with egg yolk until thick and lemon colored.

BEAT in sugar, butter, and cream. Mix baking powder with 1-1/2 cups flour, and stir into butter mixture.

STIR in enough flour so that the dough picks up all particles around the bowl.

ROLL onto a lightly floured cutting board until the dough is 1/8 inch think. Cut the dough into strips 4 x 2 inches.

CUT a slit into the center of each strip and pull through one end of the Keljner so that it resembles a bow.

HEAT oil in a heavy pan or deep fat fryer. The heat should be 375 degrees F. or hot enough to fry a small piece of bread golden brown in a minute. Carefully, drop Keljner, one at a time, into the hot fat.

FRY for 3-4 minutes, turning once. The pastries will be golden brown.

DRAIN and sprinkle with a thick coating of confectioners sugar.

Each serving: 124 calories; 13 gm carbohydrates; 2 gm protein; 7 gm fat (54% calories from fat); 30 mg cholesterol; 31 mg sodium; 25 mg potassium.

macadamia**miracles**

- non-stick cooking spray
- ½ cup butter, softened
- 1 cup brown sugar, packed
- 1 egg
- 1 cup cold Kona coffee (or strongly flavored coffee or espresso)
- 1-3/4 cups all purpose flour
- ½ teaspoon baking soda
- ½ teaspoon salt
- ½ teaspoon nutmeg
- ½ teaspoon cinnamon
- 1-1/4 cups raisins
- ½ cup macadamia nuts, chopped

kona Mountain Coffee, Inc., in Kealakekua, Hawaii, adapted this recipe to make use of local products such as kona coffee and macadamia nuts. These tasty cookies are great with coffee!

SERVES: 48

PREHEAT oven to 400 degrees F. Spray 2 baking sheets with non-stick cooking spray. In a medium-sized mixing bowl, cream butter with brown sugar and egg until the mixture is smooth.

STIR in coffee. Next, in a large mixing bowl, sift flour with soda, salt, nutmeg, and cinnamon. Stir the dry mixture into the creamed mixture.

ADD raisins and nuts. Chills for at least 4 hours.

DROP by teaspoonfuls onto lightly greased baking sheets, 2 inches apart. Bake for 8 to 10 minutes until the cookies are lightly browned.

Each serving: 71 calories; 11 gm carbohydrates; 1 gm protein; 3 gm fat (35% calories from fat); 11 mg cholesterol; 52 mg sodium; 59 mg potassium.

rose's**old-fashioned chocolate**cake

- non-stick cooking spray
- 2 cups all purpose flour, sifted
- 2 cups sugar
- ½ teaspoon salt
- 1 cup butter
- 4 tablespoons cocoa
- 1 cup water
- ½ cup buttermilk
- 1 teaspoon baking soda
- 2 eggs
- 1 teaspoon vanilla

CHOCOLATE ICING
- 3 tablespoons cocoa
- 6 tablespoons milk
- 1 pound confectioners sugar
- 1 teaspoon vanilla
- ½ cup butter
- 1 cup flaked coconut
- 1 cup pecans, chopped

This chocolate cake has won prizes all over the world! My sister-in-law, Rose Ward, recently shared the recipe with me and I adapted it adding my favorite chocolate icing.

SERVES: 24

PREHEAT oven to 350 degrees F. Spray a 9x13x4 inch rectangular loaf pan with non-stick cooking spray. In a large bowl, combine flour, sugar, and salt. Set aside. In a medium-sized saucepan, heat butter, cocoa, and water. Bring to a full boil. Pour over flour mixture.

BEAT in buttermilk, baking soda, eggs, and vanilla. Beat well. Pour into prepared pan. Bake for 30 minutes or until a toothpick inserted in the center comes out clean. Immediately frost with easy chocolate frosting. The cake is better on the second day because the icing melts into the cake…making it moist and delicious.

TO MAKE ICING: In medium-sized bowl, combine cocoa, milk, confectioners sugar, vanilla, and butter. Mix at high speed with an electric mixer. Stir in coconut and nuts.

Each serving: 339 calories; 46 gm carbohydrate; 29 gm protein; 29 gm fat (45% calories from fat); 54 mg cholesterol; 205 mg sodium; 91 mg potassium.

cinnamon**coffee**cake

- non-stick cooking spray
- 3 cups all purpose flour
- 1 teaspoon salt
- 3 tablespoons sugar
- 1 package (3/4 ounce) dry yeast
- ½ cup very warm water
- 1 egg
- 1 cup evaporated milk
- 2 tablespoons butter, melted
- ½ cup brown sugar, packed
- ¾ teaspoon cinnamon

arecipe from my past! Some 30+ years ago, my professor at Ohio State University shared this with our foods' class. It's been in my recipe file ever since. Now, I've adapted it so it's ready for the oven in 30 minutes.

SERVES: 12

SPRAY 2, 8" round baking pans with non-stick cooking spray. In a large mixing bowl, combine flour, salt, sugar and yeast.

USING an electric mixer, blend in warm water.

chapter seven

ADD egg, and ¾ of the evaporated milk. Continue mixing until smooth and satiny, about 5 minutes. Divide dough into 2 portions. Press into round pans so that dough covers all sides. Cover and allow to rise in a warm place for 20 minutes.

PREHEAT oven to 325 degrees F. Mix butter with remaining evaporated milk, brown sugar and cinnamon. With a wooden spoon handle, make indentations into the tops of prepared pans.

BRUSH and fill the indentations with brown sugar mixture.

BAKE for 25 minutes or until tops of coffee cakes are lightly browned. This coffee cake freezes and reheats well.

Each serving: 201 calories; 38 gm carbohydrates; 5 gm protein; 3 fat (12% calories from fat); 29 mg cholesterol; 216 mg sodium; 150 mg potassium.

toffee**coffee** **pecan**pie

- 3 eggs
- 1-1/2 cups brown sugar, packed
- ½ cup freshly brewed, strong coffee
- 2 tablespoons butter, melted
- 1 teaspoon vanilla
- 1 cup chocolate morsels
- 1 unbaked, 9-inch pie shell
- 1-1/2 cups pecan halves

This is so easy to make…and it's the "best ever" pecan pie!

SERVES: 16

PREHEAT oven to 450 degrees F. With an electric mixer, beat eggs, sugar, and coffee in a medium-sized bowl. Next, add butter and vanilla.

SPRINKLE chocolate morsels onto the bottom of the pie shell. Next, sprinkle pecans over the chocolate pieces. Spoon filling over chocolate and pecans.

PLACE pie into the oven for 5 minutes, then reduce the heat to 325 degrees F. and bake until well set, 25 to 30 minutes.

Each serving: 270 calories; 32 gm carbohydrates; 3 gm protein; 16 gm fat (50% calories from fat); 107 mg cholesterol; 203 mg sodium; 331 mg potassium.

Applegate, Liz. "What's brewin'?". RUNNER'S WORLD, November, 1989, pg. 22.

Anderson, Kenneth. THE POCKET GUIDE TO COFFEES AND TEAS. New York: G.P. Putnam and Sons, 1982.

Backus, Nancy. "Brew-ha-ha: good coffee sends guests away smiling." CONSUMER REPORTS, January 1991, page 31.

Barlow, Yvonne."Espresso on the run." TRAVEL-HOLIDAY, Febr., 1989, pg. 100.

Billings, John David. HARDTACK AND COFFEE. Williamstown, Mass.: Corner House Publishers, 1972.

"...but on the other hand." SCIENCE NEWS, October 20, 1990, page 253.

Castle, Timothy J. THE PERFECT CUP Reading, Mass.: Addison-Wesley Publishing Co., 1991.

"Comeback time for coffee: let's have another cup and straight this out." TIME, October 22, 1990, page 59.

COFFEE DRINKING SURVEY, London: International Coffee Organization, 1986.

Darroch, Nadina. COOKING WITH COFFEE. New York: Hart Publishing Co., 1978.

Davids, Kenneth. COFFEE. San Ramon, California: 101 Productions, 1987.

DeMers, John. THE COMMUNITY KITCHENS GUIDE TO GOURMET COFFEE. New York: Simon and Schuster, 1986.

Gorden, Jean. COFFEE: RECIPES, CUSTOMS, FACTS & FANCIES. Woodstock, Vt.: Red Rose Publications, 1963.

Ellis, Aytoun. THE PENNY UNIVERSITIES. LONDON: Secker & Warburg, 1956.

"Fewer cups, but a much richer brew." BUSINESS WEEK, November 4, 1991, page 80. Grobee, Diederick et al. "Coffee, caffeine and cardiovascular disease in men." The New England Journal of Medicine, October 11, 1990, page 1026.

Ingall, Marjorie."Now the good news about caffeine."MCCALL'S, Aug.1991,pg 18.

Jacob, Heinrick Eduard. COFFEE: THE EPIC OF A COMMODITY. New York: Viking Press, 1935.

Kaufman, William I. THE COFFEE COOKBOOK. Garden City, New York: Doubleday & Company, 1964.

Kolpas, Norman. THE COFFEE LOVERS' COMPANION. New York: Quick Fox, 1977.

Kummer, Corby. "Before the first sip: how to start a good cup of coffee." THE ATLANTIC, June, 1990, page 107.

Knapp, Caroline."Damn, that's a good coffee!"MADEMOISELLE February, 1991, pg 62.

Lingle, Ted. COFFEE CUPPERS' HANDBOOK. Washington, D.C.: The Coffee Development Group, 1987.

Loud, Lance. "Coffee and Cigarettes." AMERICAN FILM, January 1990, pg. 16.

MacKay, Barbara. "What to drink when you exercise." CHATELAINE, Jun, 1989, pg 38.

Oldenberg, Ray. THE GREAT GOOD PLACE. New York: Parragon House, 1989.

Mariani, John F. AMERICA EATS OUT. New York: Morrow, 1991.

McCoy, Elin and John Frederick Walker. COFFEE AND TEA. New York: New American Library, 1988.

Perry, Sara. THE COMPLETE COFFEE BOOK. San Francisco: Chronicle Books, 1991.

Reese, Diana. "Is coffee an aphrodisiac?" NEW CHOICES FOR THE BEST YEARS, September, 1990, page 30.

Rubin, Rita. "Good to the last drop? Coffee researchers spill the beans." AMERICAN HEALTH, September 1991, page 48.

Schwartz, Amy. THE LADY WHO PUT SALT IN HER COFFEE. San Diego: Harcourt Brace Jovanovich, 1989.

"Sex, seniors, and coffee-drinking habits." SCIENCE NEWS, February 3, 1990, pg 78.

Shafer, Charles & Violet. COFFEE. San Francisco: Yerba Buena Press, 1976.

Smith, Emily T. "Coffee drinkers have no grounds for concern." BUSINESS WEEK, October 22, 1990, page 119.

The Specialty Coffee Assocation of America: One World Trade Center, Suite 800, Long Beach, California.

The Specialty Coffee Assocation of America: 1987 Tour to Costa Rica.

Stinchecum, Amanda Mayer. "Japan's other ritual: a coffee ceremony." THE NEW YORK TIMES, November 17, 1991, section 5, page XX6.

Svicarovich, John et al. THE COFFEE BOOK. Englewood Cliffs, N.J.: Prentice Hall, Inc. 1976.

"The Taste of Fresh-Brewed." CONSUMER REPORTS, January 1991, page 30.

Terrill, Ross. "The coffee house of Li Pingfen." WORLD MONITOR, July 1989, page 34.

Ukers, William. THE ROMANCE OF COFFEE. New York: Tea and Coffee Trade Journal Co., 1948.

Ward, Mary. Media Tour: "Brewing the Perfect Cup of Coffee." Atlanta, Boston, Chicago, Cincinnati, Cleveland, Dallas, Detroit, Fresno, Houston, Los Angeles, Miami, Minneapolis, New York, Orlando, San Francisco, Seattle: Phillips Home Products, Inc., 1987.

Ward, Mary. Pamphlet: "How to Brew the Perfect Cup of Coffee." Canton, Ohio: Phillips Home Products, 1987.

index

index